Freedom Now!

Freedom Now!

FRANCINE KLAGSBRUN

The Story of the Abolitionists

HOUGHTON MIFFLIN COMPANY BOSTON 1972

FOR SARAH
who shared her first year of life
with the abolitionists.

5-10-73 *E449 .K53*

Contents

Freedom Now!

★ CHAPTER 1 ★

"Negroes for Sale"

The shrieks of the women, and the groans of the dying, rendered the whole a scene of horror almost inconceivable . . .

One day, when we had a smooth sea and moderate wind, two of my wearied countrymen who were chained together . . . preferring death to such a life of misery, somehow made through the nettings and jumped into the sea; immediately another quite dejected fellow, who, on account of his illness, was suffered to be out of irons, also followed their example; and I believe many more would very soon have done the same, if they had not been prevented by the ship's crew, who were instantly alarmed. Those of us that were the most active, were in a moment put down under the deck; and there was such a noise and confusion amongst the people of the ship as I never heard before, to stop her, and get the boat out to go after the slaves. However, two of the wretches were drowned, but they got the other, and afterwards flogged him unmercifully, for thus attempting to prefer death to slavery. In this manner we continued to undergo more hardships than I can now relate, hardships which are inseparable from this accursed trade . . .

— by Gustavus Vassa, a freed slave, writing in 1789 about his personal experiences aboard a slave ship

The institution of slavery that the abolitionists fought had become rooted in the American way of life almost four hundred years before they lived — from the time of the discovery

of the New World. Slavery was a big business in the United States. People made fortunes from buying and selling slaves and from trading in the products of slavery. Most white Americans accepted the slavery of black people without question, as the natural order of life. And it was this unquestioning acceptance, along with the institution itself, that would make the abolitionists' task of overthrowing slavery so difficult.

Europeans had started the overseas trade in black people. Before it would end, about ten million African men, women, and children would be carried away from their homes to lands they had never dreamed existed.

The Europeans shipped slaves to their colonies in the New World to clear the land and mine gold and other precious metals. They found blacks the ideal workers for their new lands. The native Indians became ill too easily with the white man's diseases. And poor whites, sent as servants from Europe to America, often ran away before fulfilling their working terms. The black men were strong and healthy. Because of their color, they could be spotted easily if they tried to escape. And they were available.

Africa had slaves long before white men came to buy them. Black kings and chieftains kept prisoners taken in war as their slaves. When Europeans created a demand for slaves, the African chieftains competed with one another in supplying them. Tribe raided tribe to capture able-bodied men, women, and children for the marketplace. Villages were often pirated in the middle of the night, and their victims marched off in chains to be sold to the white man.

The slave-trading nations kept slave posts along the African coast. Here, ships laden with goods to barter came to make their exchange. The Europeans gave the Africans arms, gun-powder, tallow, cloth, liquor, and beads as payment for their people. Traders would go from port to port to buy their human cargo. At each stop they examined the wares carefully, search-ing for young, strong men and for women sturdy enough to bear many slave children.

The slave ships' voyages from Africa to America became known as the "middle passage." It was a passage of suffering, sorrow, and deadly sickness. The slave ships were designed to hold as many slaves as possible in the smallest amount of space. The slave area in the lower deck was carefully measured so that the slaves could lie side by side, naked and chained together by their ankles. In one ship, the space given each slave was five feet, six inches long and eighteen inches high. This allowed a man to lie down, but not to sit up or even turn around.

During most of the trip, the slaves were kept below deck, packed tightly together with little air to breathe and little water to drink. In their misery, some killed others to give themselves more air and more space. Other slaves jumped overboard at the first chance, preferring suicide to the horrors on board and the terrors that lay ahead. Many other captives died with great suffering of diseases that attacked them during the long voyages.

When a slaver finally reached its destination, purchasers from the area swarmed around to inspect the goods. They felt muscles, looked at teeth, measured legs, and carefully examined naked bodies. After they settled on a price, they marched their new property off to be branded with the mark of their owners. Then the slaves were seasoned into their new way of life and were quickly expected to carry their burden of labor.

A Dutch man-of-war brought the first blacks to the North

American colony of Jamestown, Virginia, in 1619. The Dutch captain sold his twenty African "negars" as servants rather than slaves. Like indentured white servants, they were to serve out a period of time by working for their masters and then were to receive their freedom. Blacks who came to other colonies had the same status at first. Soon, however, they were reduced from servants to slaves bound for life.

As the colonies grew, the need for laborers increased. The Southern colonies especially needed many hands to produce the tobacco, rice, and other crops that they grew on their plantations. More and more black Africans were imported. By the end of the 1600s, thousands of black slaves lived and worked in the American colonies. In some Southern colonies they outnumbered whites.

The large number of these slaves alarmed white colonists. News of bloody uprisings in other parts of the Americas, and some attempted rebellions in the colonies themselves, led the colonists to pass strict slave laws to govern them. The South, with its growing number of blacks, had the harshest laws.

In the Northern colonies slaves worked in shops or in homes. Mostly, however, Northerners, like European slave traders, were interested in slaves as merchandise for trade and exchange. During the 1700s and early 1800s, some of the greatest fortunes in New England were built around the slave trade. Less than a hundred years later descendants of those New England slave traders would lead the struggle to abolish slavery.

New England merchants grew wealthy by following what became known as "triangular trade routes." In New England, the colonists loaded their ships with food, fish, lumber, and manufactured goods. They carried these goods to the West Indies, where they exchanged the goods for molasses and sugar. Then they carried these commodities back to New England to be made into rum. The traders carried the rum to Africa. Along with trinkets, beads, and cloth, they traded the rum for slaves. Back across the middle passage they went with their cargo of slaves, which they sold in the West Indies and the Southern colonies in return for more sugar and molasses.

Like other merchants, the New England slave traders advertised their wares, using glowing terms and hard-sell techniques. Newspapers throughout the colonies carried ads for "NEGROES FOR SALE." An ad might announce a "cargo of very fine stout Men and Women, in good order and fit for immediate service," or a "parcel of fine Negro boys and girls," or a "very likely Negro boy lately imported."

By the time of the American Revolution, more than 700,000 blacks lived in the American colonies. By then, most Northerners had found it unprofitable to keep slaves. One by one, after the Revolution, Northern states began to abolish slavery, some immediately, and some on a more gradual basis. Vermont was the first state to abolish slavery, in 1777.

Doing away with slavery did not mean, however, that Northerners liked black people or even respected them. Most Northerners, like Southerners, considered the black man inferior to the white man. They treated blacks somewhat as they might treat children, as though they were simple-minded and incapable of assuming responsibility. Northern whites had little to do with the free blacks who lived among them, hiring the men only in the lowest-paying jobs and employing the women as domestic servants. Even many people who actively opposed slavery found it impossible to accept black people as their equal, socially or intellectually.

Slavery continued to grow in the Southern states during the 1700s, and the slave trade continued to flourish. Southerners used the "fact" of black inferiority as the basis for their pro-slavery arguments. With no knowledge of the achievements of African history, they pointed to the supposed backwardness of Africa as proof that blacks could not rise to the level of Western civilization. Servitude was good for blacks, they maintained, because it helped civilize them, and contact with Christianity exposed the "heathen" to the influence of religion.

After the invention of the cotton gin in 1793 the need for slaves in the South increased more than ever. The price of cotton fell, the demand for it rose, and Southerners grew huge crops of cotton on their ever-expanding plantations. They wanted hands — black hands — to pick and separate the cotton as quickly as possible.

Hardly anybody noticed it when the slave trade was abolished in 1808. Officials closed their eyes to the illegal hordes of slaves now smuggled into the country. If anything, conditions became worse on slave ships. Built for speed, the ships gave slaves even less space than before. And to avoid being caught, the slave captains might even dump their cargoes of black slaves ino the ocean when spotted by government patrols. The illegal African slave trade continued almost to the days of the Civil War.

Along with the African trade, a brisk domestic trade moved blacks from one state to another. Businessmen sold slaves together with other merchandise, such as animals and farm supplies. Charity organizations considered slaves a fine prize for raffle holders. Many slaveholders tried to keep families together when selling their slaves. But if they could get a good price for selling individual members, they often did not hesitate to do so.

Some slave owners tried to breed slaves and sell them for money, much the way they might breed cattle. They encouraged women slaves to have many children and even rewarded them whenever they gave birth. Some slave girls became mothers at the age of fourteen or fifteen to provide their masters with babies whom they could sell for as much as $200. And young women with children — called "rattlin' good breeders" — sold high at slave auctions in the hopes that they would produce more wealth for their masters.

By the 1800s, slavery was the South's own "peculiar institution," carefully regulated by rules and traditions. Earlier slave codes became hardened as word of new revolts in Haiti and other Caribbean Islands left Southerners fearful for their lives. The codes differed from state to state. But at the bottom of them all was the view of slaves as property and the desire to keep them dependent on their masters. The laws stated that slaves could not leave their plantations without written permission. They forbade slaves to own property or to buy and sell goods. They forbade them to own firearms of any sort. They did not permit them to visit the homes of whites or of free blacks. They restricted slaves from making contracts or offering testimony in court. They made it a crime, sometimes punishable by death, for a slave to strike a white person, even in self-defense.

How strictly these rules were obeyed depended on each slave

owner. Some masters were extremely cruel. Many others were kind and considerate of their slaves. But whether a master was kind or cruel, whether a slave lived well or badly, did not change the institution of slavery.

★ CHAPTER 2 ★

Early Opponents of Slavery

There is a saying that we should do to all men as we would
be done to ourselves . . . Here is liberty of conscience which
is right and reasonable; here ought to be likewise liberty of
the body . . .

. . . Pray, what thing in the world can be done worse toward us, than if men should rob or steal us away and sell
us for slaves to strange countries . . .

. . . have these poor Negroes not as much right to fight for
their freedom as you have to keep them slaves?
— First known protest against slavery in America by
Quakers in Germantown, Pennsylvania, in 1688

★

The Quakers were the first people to protest as a group
against slavery. These gentle folk, who called themselves the
Society of Friends, fashioned their daily lives on their religious
convictions. In England, where their religion began, they had
been severely persecuted for those convictions and many had
migrated to the New World. There, they disregarded the
rituals of established churches and followed simple religious
practices, emphasizing above everything else the dignity of
man. At first, Quakers in America owned slaves and some
grew rich from the slave trade. Under the influence of their
religious leaders, however, they soon came to regard slavery as

a sin. Even before the American Revolution, most Quaker slaveholders had begun to free their slaves.

One of the Quaker leaders, the hunchbacked Benjamin Lay, had his own way of impressing his coreligionists with the horrors of slavery. He kidnaped their children and hid them for a while so that they could learn for themselves the anguish slave parents felt when their children were torn from them and sold into bondage.

More conventional but even more influential than Lay were two other Quaker leaders, John Woolman and Anthony Benezet. Woolman, a tailor by trade, traveled throughout America and England, writing about slavery, meeting with people, and discussing the moral wrongs of the slave system in gentle, persuasive tones. His warm, almost saintlike personality won him many friends and followers. More an organizer and propagandist than Woolman, Benezet circulated antislavery pamphlets and reprinted the writings of Europeans who opposed slavery.

Later, abolitionists would regard the works of Woolman, Benezet, Lay, and other Quakers as sacred literature from which they quoted freely. The abolitionists would have much in common with the early Quakers. Their actions, too, would stem from strong religious beliefs and they would make the sinfulness of slavery the core of their antislavery arguments. Like the Quakers, the abolitionists would suffer persecutions and insults in practicing and preaching their antislavery creed. Ironically, after the abolitionists began their militant attacks on slavery, the Quakers withdrew from the battle and refused to link themselves with the fiery language and aggressive behavior of abolitionists.

Urged on by Benjamin Franklin, the Pennsylvania Friends organized America's first antislavery society in 1775. Later it was incorporated under a wordy title that left no doubt about its purpose: The Pennsylvania Society for Promoting the Abolition of Slavery, the Relief of Free Negroes Unlawfully Held in Bondage, and for Improving the Condition of the African Race. Franklin became the first president of the Pennsylvania Society. Antislavery societies that came afterward followed the practice of using long names, perhaps to give themselves more prestige in serving an unpopular cause.

As time went on, Quakers in other states organized antislavery societies. Two friends, Elihu Embree and Charles Osborn, built an antislavery society in Tennessee around 1814, one of the first such societies in the South. Embree published the *Manumission Intelligencer* and later the *Emancipator,* the first American periodicals devoted exclusively to antislavery issues. Osborn moved from Tennessee to Ohio, where he published the *Philanthropist,* dealing with antislavery and other reform movements.

With all their good works, the Quakers did not have a monopoly on antislavery activities. Men and women of many faiths involved themselves in trying to better the lot of the black people in America. More than seventy-five years before the American Revolution, Judge Samuel Sewall of Massachusetts wrote one of the first published arguments against slavery. In his pamphlet, *The Selling of Joseph,* he used the Biblical story of Joseph in Egypt to point out the wrongs of slavery. The pamphlet became a source of Biblical arguments against slavery for the abolitionists. The antislavery people would find, however, that the Bible could be interpreted in many ways and that proslavery people also would back up their position with Biblical quotations.

During the Revolutionary period, a number of Founding Fathers spoke out against slavery. Benjamin Franklin, George Washington, Thomas Jefferson, Alexander Hamilton, and others condemned the cruelty of trading in human flesh. Under their prodding, men and women who had given little thought to the plight of the slave began to see a contradiction in their struggle for freedom from Great Britain during the American Revolution and their denial of freedom to black people.

Although Jefferson himself was a Virginia slave owner, he included a section denouncing slavery and the slave trade in the Declaration of Independence. But pressure from Southern slave owners and Northern slave merchants led to the deletion of Jefferson's antislavery section from the Declaration of Independence before it was adopted in 1776.

Later, when Jefferson drafted the Ordinance of 1784, he called for the prohibition of slavery in all new territories, including those in the Southwest. Again, proslavery forces caused Jefferson's writing to be changed, so that when the Northwest Ordinance became law in 1787 slavery was forbidden only in a more limited area — the Northwest Territory, which was to become the heart of the American Midwest.

The differences between the ideals of freedom and democracy that the Founding Fathers spoke about and the legal documents upon which they built the new nation would become a sore point for those who later dedicated themselves to destroying slavery. In spite of its omissions, the Declaration of Independence did proclaim that "all men are created equal," and on this statement abolitionists of another era would base many of their antislavery arguments. The Constitution offered them far less to go on. All down the line, it compromised on the slavery issue. Instead of abolishing the slave trade as some of the Founding Fathers urged, it allowed the African trade to continue for twenty years longer. It stated that all runaway slaves must be returned to their masters. And it counted a slave as only three fifths of a person. That meant that slave states could count three fifths of their slaves as part of their population in determining how many representatives in Congress they would have. These compromises between the goals of freedom and the pressures of slaveholding interests would make the Constitution the most disputed document of the pre–Civil War period.

In the early days of the Republic, a number of distinguished statesmen continued in the antislavery tradition of Franklin and Jefferson. Benjamin Rush, a well-known physician who had signed the Declaration of Independence, published several antislavery pamphlets. He went out of his way to make the acquaintance of free blacks, even exchanging medical information with a former slave who became a physician. John Jay, chief justice of the United States, helped found the New York Society for Promoting the Manumission of Slaves and served as its first president. Alexander Hamilton was its second president. Ezra Stiles, first president of Yale College, also presided over an antislavery society, the Connecticut Society for the Promotion of Freedom.

The antislavery societies founded by these leading citizens published pamphlets to convince slaveholders that free labor was more profitable than slave labor and to arouse public opinion against slavery. Members set up committees to find jobs for free blacks and schools to educate them. One of the

American Negro school

societies' most important services was advising blacks on their legal rights and working to free those men and women who had been kidnaped or held illegally as slaves. As much as they could, society members boycotted slave products. They tried to buy "free cotton" grown on plantations that did not use slave labor. Their records include recipes for making sugar and molasses so that these products would not have to be imported from the slaveholding West Indies.

Opponents of slavery liked to feel that their efforts brought about the limitations on slavery included in the Missouri Compromise of 1820. When the territory of Missouri applied for statehood, it opened a problem that would swell into one of the most feverish issues of the pre–Civil War days. The problem concerned the extension of slavery into new territories that became part of the United States. Southerners, who wanted to increase their representation in Congress, favored permitting slavery in all new territories. Northerners who opposed slavery and others who feared Southern expansion wanted to keep slavery out of the territories. The Missouri Compromise admitted Missouri as a slave state, but to keep the balance of power it also admitted Maine as a free state. In addition, it excluded slavery from all territories except Missouri that lay north of the parallel 36° 30′, which was the southern boundary of Missouri, a victory for antislavery forces.

For many of the men and women who took up the antislavery cause during the early and middle 1800s, black freedom was one of several reforms to which they devoted their energies. The 1800s were the heyday of reform movements. The expansion of the Western frontier and the spread of democracy focused the nation's attention on the individual and his rights. At the same time, religious reform movements — themselves reflecting the spirit of freedom and individualism — gave new perspectives to old religious views. Churches began to emphasize good works and concern for others rather than strict rituals and orthodox doctrines. Influenced by the changes about them, Americans began to look closely at their society, to try to help, and change, and do things for it. Prison reform, care for the insane, universal public education, aid for the blind, peace movements, women's rights, temperance — all attracted the interests of thinking men and women. It was a logical step for these same men and women to turn their attention to the blacks, the most repressed members of society.

Unlike the later abolitionists, however, these early opponents of slavery did not see their work as a crusade to change the structure of society. They wished only to make life easier for the black man, to give him some of the dignity that they believed was the natural right of all men. Most accepted the traditional idea of black inferiority. They did not seek immediate freedom for slaves or equality for the black people. They called for the abolition of the domestic slave trade and for gradual emancipation with payment to slaveholders for the loss of their property. They spoke in moderate terms, unwilling to anger Southern masters or Northern businessmen. In all that they said and did, they counseled slaves to be patient and forbearing.

Thomas Jefferson summed up the attitude and confusion of white reformers when he wrote, "Nothing is more certainly written in the book of fate, than that these people are to be free; nor is it less certain that the two races, equally free, cannot live in the same government."

★ CHAPTER 3 ★

Rebellions and Reactions

Are we men!! I ask you . . . Are we MEN? Did our creator
make us to be slaves to dust and ashes like ourselves? . . .
How we could be so *submissive* to a gang of men, whom
we cannot tell whether they are as good as ourselves or not,
I never conceive . . . America is more our country than it
is the whites — we have enriched it with our *blood and
tears* . . .

Remember, Americans, that we must and shall be free
and enlightened as you are, will you wait until we shall,
under God, obtain our liberty by the crushing arm of
power? . . . wo, wo, will be to you if we have to obtain our
freedom by fighting . . .

— DAVID WALKER, a free black, in his *Appeal,* 1829

★

lways just below the surface in the American South lay
the fear of slave uprisings. That fear cut away at the comforts
and rewards slaveholders found in their peculiar institution.
And that fear would lead Southerners to react violently to the
abolitionists, whose words they would interpret as a rallying
cry for rebels. During the early 1800s, while reformers worked
to ease the black situation, slaveholders tried to protect themselves from uprisings by passing ever-stricter laws limiting the
rights of black people.

Southern whites maintained control over the blacks who

lived among them in several ways. As much as they could, they kept their slaves uneducated, most without any knowledge of reading or writing. They made slaves almost completely dependent on their masters by impressing upon them the idea that they were inferior to whites and incapable of taking care of themselves. And they backed their power with force. Private patrolmen, local policemen, and state militia stood ready to go into action at the first sign of slave unrest. Slaves knew, and were reminded again and again, that rebellion had little chance of succeeding and that the penalty for attempted insurrection was death.

Most slaves lived within the rules set out for them. When they fought the system, they did it in subtle, quiet ways. Many of them established a slow, easygoing work pace, irritating white masters with their laziness. They destroyed tools and equipment, pretending that they didn't understand how to use these materials. "Accidentally," they set fire to their masters' fields and homes. And, of course, they ran away. One Southern physician, Dr. Samuel Cartwright, published his diagnoses of two diseases that he said were peculiar to slaves. The disease of "drapetomania", he explained, caused them to run away. It was an illness of the mind that could sometimes be cured by "whipping the devil out of them." The other exclusive slave disease, which Cartwright called "dysaethesia aethiopica," caused slaves to "break, waste, and destroy everything they handled." This disease, he solemnly explained, "appears as if intentional," but actually comes from "stupidness of mind and insensibility of nerves induced by the disease." For many black slaves, this "stupidness" was the cleverest way they knew to resist their condition.

For some slaves, however, passive resistance was not enough. These people were willing to risk everything in open rebellion to gain freedom for themselves and their people. Sometimes they were driven by the desperate knowledge that they had no other way to break their bondage. Sometimes they were motivated by a desire for revenge so strong that they were willing to sacrifice their own lives to snuff out the lives of white men. And sometimes they were inspired by a mystical belief in themselves as the instruments of God to deliver their people from captivity.

Slave rebellions had been part of slavery in America from the beginning. At least 250 conspiracies and revolts took place from colonial times until the Civil War. In colonial New York, New Orleans, Charleston, and towns throughout America, blacks acting alone or in groups — and sometimes with the aid of poor whites — plotted to destroy their masters. Many of the plots were discovered before the revolts got under way, but in a number of cases, whites were murdered or injured before an uprising was quelled.

An atmosphere of rebellion hung over Southern regions during the Revolutionary War period when word of a successful insurrection in the West Indian colony of Santo Domingo reached American slaves. Blacks in Santo Domingo had massacred the white population and eventually set up their own colony of Haiti. Rumors, eyewitness accounts, and plans based on those of Santo Domingo circulated through the black grapevine. Whites reacted to the restlessness among the blacks by tightening the codes that regulated black behavior, keeping alert — and waiting.

In the summer of 1800, a shudder of horror rolled through

the slaveholding states, and the fears that had been growing steadily for years focused on one Gabriel, the slave of Thomas Prosser, in Henrice County, Virginia. This towering, six-foot-two rebel had worked out detailed plans to capture Richmond, the capital of Virginia, and from there begin a massive slave revolt. His wife and two brothers had helped him recruit followers, and throughout the spring of 1800 the conspirators had made swords, bayonets, and bullets. At the last minute, two slaves who had heard of the plot told their master, and he, in turn, informed James Monroe, then governor of Virginia. Monroe sent armed troops to the capital and informed every militia commander in the state. By the time the troops arrived, about a thousand slaves had gathered several miles outside of Charleston, armed with their crude, homemade weapons. The troops and a sudden, violent rainstorm that flooded roads and bridges forced the rebels to disband.

Dozens of blacks were arrested during the next few days. Gabriel tried to escape by stowing away on a schooner, but he was recognized in Norfolk and brought back in chains. Along with some thirty other slaves he was condemned to hang. With the others, he died silently, revealing nothing of the extent of his plans or the persons involved.

Gabriel's revolt, like the conspiracies that came before it, led Southerners to take new measures to restrict and control the black people in their midst. Slaves were no longer permitted to be hired out to work on other peoples' lands. They were forbidden to gather for meetings. White persons found teaching them to read or write could be jailed and fined. There were other laws, each adding new limitations on black people. But the laws could not control the restlessness that was everywhere

in the slave states after Gabriel's revolt. Nor could they stop
an even more frightening rebellion just twenty-two years later.
This rebellion was the work of a freeman, Denmark Vesey.

Vesey had used money won in a lottery to buy his freedom.
He worked as a carpenter in Charleston, South Carolina, where
he had managed to gather a considerable amount of property.
He could read and write and spoke several languages. White
slaveholders pointed to him as one of the more advanced of
his race, proof of their argument that contact with whites had
civilized the African savages. Certainly from talking to or
looking at Vesey, they would never have guessed that this
bearded man in his late fifties was planning to slaughter
them all.

Vesey spent years mapping out his plan, which called for the
capture of Charleston and the destruction of all its whites.
From there, he and his followers would move on to other cities,
freeing their brethren as they went. Carefully, he laid the
groundwork for his revolt. First, he gathered a handful of
trustworthy followers. There were Rolla and Ned, both slaves
of Governor Thomas Bennett of South Carolina. There were
Peter Poyas and Mingo Harth, artisans and strong, intelligent
men. There was Gullah Pritchard, feared by blacks and many
whites because of his supposed powers of witchcraft. There
were others, each chosen, admitted a white man later, with
"great penetration and sound judgment."

At night, Vesey held meetings with his recruits. He read to
them, explained one rebel, "from the Bible *how the children
of Israel were delivered out of Egypt from bondage.*" And he
worked out the details of his plans with them. They would
strike on the second Sunday in July 1822. There would be five

attacks at five different points at once. A sixth group would patrol the streets on horseback. In the meantime, the rebels would construct pike heads and gather bayonets. And they would go quietly about the plantations in the area and rouse other slaves to join their cause.

Vesey warned his followers to be cautious about discussing their plans with domestic slaves. Domestics, who lived in the masters' houses, were too loyal to their white owners and too ready to accept gifts and rewards for their loyalty.

The plans seemed foolproof. Yet this plot, like Gabriel's, was stopped by the betrayal of black men. One of the conspirators carelessly described the plans to an unsympathetic household slave. The slave told his master, who sent word to the authorities. Within days, the would-be revolution was over. A hundred and thirty-nine blacks of Charleston were rounded up and arrested. A trial found thirty-nine of them guilty and thirty-seven condemned to die, among them Peter Poyas, Mingo Harth, and Vesey himself.

"Die silent, as you shall see me do," Peter Poyas told the others. They followed his example, and the executions shed little light on the extent of the plot. Some people guessed that as many as 9000 men, including some whites, were involved.

Vesey accomplished one goal. He left the people of South Carolina terrified, and their terror spread to other slaveholders. If a war of nerves could overthrow slavery, Vesey and the other slave rebels had chosen their method wisely. But Southerners reacted to the tensions within them by passing new laws and new restrictions on black people.

Perhaps more than anything, Southerners were bothered by the fact that Vesey was a freeman. Free blacks were a thorn in the side of the South. They represented a threat to the slave system, a goal toward which all slaves might reach out. Through dozens of laws, Southern states tried to prevent whites from freeing their slaves and to keep freemen from enjoying the rights of white people. In a number of states, slaves who gained their freedom had to leave the state within a short period of time or they would be forced back into slavery. States that permitted free blacks required that they carry passes or certificates of freedom, and usually forbade them from traveling about the area or going from one state to another. When a freeman like Vesey started trouble, Southerners felt convinced that all free blacks were untrustworthy, and that their number and activities must be strictly limited.

Almost from the time slavery began in America there were free blacks in the country. Some of the first who came as indentured servants worked out their time and earned their freedom before black slavery became a fixed institution. Some were freed during the Revolutionary War period, when the spirit of freedom and democracy moved many Southerners as well as Northerners. The children of these early free blacks remained free. Other blacks managed to save enough money to buy their freedom. Some, also, were freed upon the death of their masters, according to instructions in the masters' wills. In 1790, about 59,000 free blacks lived in the United States. By 1830, the number had climbed to 319,000 — compared to more than 2,000,000 blacks who remained as slaves.

Early opponents of slavery, seeking ways to end the institution in America, knew that the free black man was the biggest stumbling block to emancipation. Southerners would never agree to the presence of thousands of freed slaves in their midst, threatening to outnumber and overwhelm them. Nor would Northerners welcome a flood of freed blacks into their states, offering competition to white laborers and artisans.

During the years when Denmark Vesey was planning his revolt, antislavery people were putting forth a solution to the problem of the free blacks designed to satisfy whites everywhere and to rid the country of troublemakers like Vesey. The plan called for slaves to be freed gradually and then sent back to Africa. In 1817, the American Colonization Society (with such well-known statesmen as James Monroe and Henry Clay among its founders) was organized to resettle former slaves and other freemen. Within a short time, almost every state had its own branch of the colonization society. By 1820, the society sent its first shipload of eighty-eight blacks to the West Coast of Africa, and two years later, it founded the colony of Liberia, especially for freed blacks. Within ten years, about 1400 freemen had been settled in Liberia.

Southerners as well as Northerners welcomed the Colonization Society. Slaveholders saw it as a way of ridding themselves of the annoying free blacks and making slavery more secure. Some, who felt kindly toward their slaves, were happy to be able to free them and send them out of the country where they would not face the danger of becoming enslaved again. Northerners who wanted to help blacks felt sure that the colonization plan would gradually bring about the emancipation of them all. Less idealistic colonizationists, guided by race prejudice, thought it best to return blacks to the primitive conditions of their native lands because, they believed, blacks would never be able to fit into Western society.

The only people who did not like the colonization plan were

the free blacks for whom it was intended. Everywhere, in churches, meeting halls, and homes, blacks gathered to state their case to white America. They were Americans and this was their home. They did not want to be shipped off to a land most of them had never seen, nor did they want to turn their backs on their brothers in slavery. Mostly, they resented the attitude behind colonization, the belief in black inferiority.

Instead of exile, free blacks preferred to organize, and to fight slavery from within. During the early 1800s, while whites formed their antislavery societies — to which no blacks were admitted — those excluded established their own societies. By 1830, they had about fifty societies whose members constantly sent petitions to the government calling for the beginning of emancipation. As much as they could, free blacks helped slaves escape, often at the risk of being retaken themselves. They saved their money to buy slaves whom they could turn loose in the free states. And they published their own anti-slavery newspapers. The first black newspaper, *Freedom's Journal,* included illustrations and detailed descriptions of cruelty to slaves. In the first issue, published in 1827, editors John Russwurm and Samuel E. Cornish cried out, "Too long have others spoken for us. Too long has the publick been deceived by misrepresentations."

Some free blacks, like Denmark Vesey, carried their fight far beyond the bounds of antislavery societies. Seven years after the Vesey conspiracy, the revolt of another freeman, a revolt in writing this time, caused new alarm in the South. The revolt took the form of a seventy-six-page pamphlet so fiery and alarming that it was read and reread throughout the North and South. Its title alone took up a good part of a page: *Walk-*

er's Appeal in Four Articles Together with a Preamble to the Colored Citizens of the World, But in Particular and Very Expressly to those of the United States. David Walker, its author, had moved in 1828 from North Carolina to Boston, where he earned his living by buying and selling secondhand clothes. He became active in the Massachusetts General Colored Association, a black antislavery society. After he published his *Appeal* in 1829, he became known far beyond Boston's black society.

David Walker's *Appeal* called on blacks to take direct action to throw off the yoke of their servitude. "Are we men!!" he cried out. "Are we MEN?" In page after page, he threatened white America and pleaded with his people to fight their bondage like men.

Walker managed to distribute his pamphlet in many areas, including the South, where a group in Georgia offered $1000 reward for his head and $10,000 for taking him alive. These offers were the beginning of a pattern that would become common in later years when sums of money were offered for key abolitionist leaders.

Walker died suddenly, mysteriously, in 1830. Exactly how is not known, although some said he was poisoned. Long after his death his pamphlet continued to stir black readers and infuriate whites.

A new black revolt began a year after Walker's death. This one had a more profound effect on the South and on the nation as a whole than any that came before it. Its leader, Nat Turner, would become a symbol for all time of the black man who tried to end slavery with desperate violence.

A slave preacher, Turner had studied the Bible carefully and

Nat Turner and his confederates in conference

had become convinced that he was "ordained for some great purpose in the hands of the Almighty." All he needed was a sign from God to take on the struggle of his people. That sign came to him, he believed, on February 12, 1831, when a solar eclipse blackened the sky. Along with four other men whom he took into his confidence, he decided to lead an all-out rebellion on the Fourth of July, the nation's Independence Day. The rebellion would start at his master's home in Southampton, Virginia.

Turner was sick on the "sacred day," and, after another "sign," the men chose August 21 as the day to fulfill their mission. They began by murdering Turner's master, Joseph Travis, and his family, five in all. Later, Turner described Travis as a "kind master," who "placed the greatest confidence in me; in fact I had no cause to complain of his treatment to me." That description and the treatment the "kind master" received from a slave bent on freedom horrified Southerners almost as much as the rebellion itself.

From the Travis home, the band moved on to other plantations, slaughtering whites and gathering black recruits as they went along. At the end of twenty-four hours they had seventy rebels in their group. Behind them they had left a bloody trail of sixty dead white men, women, and children.

Turner's band marched toward the county seat of Jerusalem, where they hoped to get arms. They were stopped, first, by a volunteer corps of whites. Later a company of militia and state troops routed them completely. A sweeping massacre of blacks followed and more than a hundred slaves in the area were killed. Turner managed to escape and hide in a cave for six weeks until one Benjamin Phipps caught him. He was armed only with an old sword and surrendered immediately.

While waiting in prison for his trial, Nat Turner told his story to Thomas R. Gray, who published it as a pamphlet under the title *The Confessions of Nat Turner, the Leader of the Late Insurrection in Southampton, Va.* The *Confessions* were presented as evidence before the court that tried him and condemned him to hang. In spite of his confessions to Gray, Turner pleaded not guilty because, he explained, he did not *feel* guilty.

The South reacted to Nat Turner's rebellion with a panic and anger beyond any that had been felt before. Southern states passed the most repressive black codes in their history. Many states outlawed free blacks from entering their territories, although Turner had been a slave. Slaves and freemen were forbidden to gather to hold religious services, and no slave or free black was permitted to preach by day or night to other blacks. In addition, they were not allowed to possess weapons of any sort, and no one was allowed to sell liquor to or buy from blacks.

Far more important than the laws, however, were the unusual debates the rebellion set off in the Virginia legislature; the topic: whether to abolish slavery from the state. Those who introduced the issue did not have great antislavery sympathies. They were more concerned with protecting themselves and their families from the menace of rebellion. They were backed by farmers and poor whites of western Virginia who did not hold slaves. The debates, between 1831 and 1832, were heated. But the proposal for emancipation was finally squelched and the legislature turned its attention to ways of ridding the state of its free blacks. The lawmakers agreed a year later to set aside state funds to support the efforts of the Colonization Society to resettle blacks in Africa.

Proslavery forces had won a major victory, not only in Virginia, but in all of the South. A new era began. The few antislavery workers who had stayed in the South over the years now left or became totally silent. Southerners began to lump all antislavery activity in the same category of violence as a Turner rebellion or a Walker *Appeal* and to react to antislavery arguments with almost as much vehemence as they reacted to slave uprisings. At this point in the North the abolition movement was about to be born.

★ CHAPTER 4 ★

A New Leader Is Heard

I *will be* as harsh as truth, and as uncompromising as justice. On this subject, I do not wish to think, or speak, or write, with moderation. No! no! Tell a man, whose house is on fire, to give a moderate alarm; tell him to moderately rescue his wife from the hands of the ravisher; tell the mother to gradually extricate her babe from the fire into which it has fallen; but urge me not to use moderation in a cause like the present. I am in earnest — I will not equivocate — I will not excuse — I will not retreat a single inch — AND I WILL BE HEARD.

— WILLIAM LLOYD GARRISON
in the first issue of the *Liberator,* 1831

In the midst of the slave rebellions and the slaveholders' reactions, a new voice was heard. It was a voice from the North, a grating, threatening uncompromising voice that was deafening in its attacks on slavery. The man who spoke with that voice would be accused by some of instigating David Walker's *Appeal,* influencing Nat Turner's rebellion, and forcing the South into its unwavering stand against emancipation. He would be credited by others with leading a weak antislavery movement into a new phase, an angry, active phase, in which nothing short of the immediate and total abolition of slavery would be acceptable. The man was William Lloyd Garrison.

Garrison burst upon the antislavery scene in 1831 with the publication of the first issue of his antislavery newspaper, the *Liberator*. In his opening editorial, he served notice to slaveholders, to colonizationists, and to mild-mannered reformers that the time for moderation on the slavery issue had passed and that he was now declaring all-out war. That war would continue for the next thirty years. Others would join Garrison in battle, but his name would always be most closely associated with the militant abolition movement that began to pound away at slavery during the 1830s. Throughout his own lifetime and long afterward, he would remain the most controversial figure of that movement.

Garrison was a man of his times. The reform movements that occupied Americans captured his imagination and inspired dedication on his part to many causes. The religious revivals that washed like waves across the country in the first part of the 1800s caught him up and gave direction to his own strong religious beliefs. The desire for reform combined with religious idealism turned his antislavery goals into a moral crusade to convert his countrymen.

The second son of a shiftless father and a religious, often self-righteous mother, Garrison never seemed to get enough attention as a child. In his adult life he was driven by a need for recognition and the desire to be heard. Yet he sought the recognition he so desperately wanted by taking up unpopular causes, as though inwardly afraid to compete in more conventional areas. Once committed to a cause, he hammered away with unquestioning certainty, convinced of his rightfulness and at the same time fearful of looking beyond himself.

For Garrison, as for other reformers, antislavery quickly

became the issue of the age. As his involvement in that cause grew, his words became piercing and his tone increasingly urgent. He didn't hesitate to describe slavery's defenders as "beasts" and "sinners," or to call an opponent a "murderous liar," or a "cruel monster." He didn't hesitate to take on the government, the churches, business interests, and other members of the Establishment in his single-minded battle.

Later, critics would wonder how much Garrison might have achieved had he not presented himself as a fanatic, had he lowered his voice and opened his mind to viewpoints other than his own. And yet, he was *heard,* and the harshness of his voice shocked some people out of the indifference that was slavery's best ally.

In his middle years, Garrison appeared every bit the reformer. Of average height, he looked out at the world through proper, steel-rimmed glasses. His face was clean shaven and his head large and shiny bald. In personal conversation he spoke in mild, scholarly tones, reserving his wrath for written editorials.

He was born in Newburyport, Massachusetts, in 1805. Three years later, Garrison's father deserted his wife and three children, leaving them poverty stricken. Garrison's mother supported her family by doing housework. As soon as he was old enough, Lloyd, as people called him, went about town peddling homemade candies and other goods.

The youth had little formal education. After short apprenticeships to a shoemaker and then a cabinetmaker, he was apprenticed at the age of thirteen to the editor of the *Newburyport Herald*. He became an expert printer and exercised his writing skills in a conversational column called "An Old Bachelor." When he completed his seven-year apprenticeship

William Lloyd Garrison

at the age of twenty, he set himself up as owner, editor, and printer of the *Newburyport Free Press*. He immediately launched into attacks on various political figures, shaping causes out of issues in which most people had little interest. The unknown young man of poor background was determined to gain a reputation quickly among the elite of New England. His time had not yet come, however, and within a year his press collapsed.

He did accomplish one important thing with the *Free Press*. He discovered the poet John Greenleaf Whittier. Without Whittier's knowledge, the poet's sister slipped one of his poems, "The Exile's Departure," under Garrison's door one day, signing it only "W." Garrison traced the poet, who was then serving as a shoemaker's apprentice, and encouraged him to write other poems. The shy Quaker Whittier and the opinionated, puritanical Garrison became good friends. Later, when Garrison became involved in antislavery, he drew Whittier into the battle with him. Even in their mature years, when they came to disagree on methods, Whittier continued to admire his first supporter.

With the collapse of his paper in 1826, Garrison moved to Boston to seek work as a printer. There he came into contact with men whose ideas would stamp themselves on his own thinking.

One of the key influences in Boston was Lyman Beecher, pastor of the Hanover Street Church, whose daughter, Harriet Beecher Stowe, would become world known for her *Uncle Tom's Cabin*. Beecher preached an evangelical religion, calling on Christians to repent immediately, return to Christ, and reform their ways. His religious philosophy was based on the idea that man had freedom to choose his actions, good or evil. In fiery, military language, he ran revival meetings and won converts from among Boston's middle-class merchants, artisans, and professional people. Soon Garrison would turn against Beecher, as he did other early influences in his life. For now, his soul warmed to Beecher's cry for Christian benevolence, an involvement in good works and in moral reforms. Beecher's church became a second home to Garrison.

Another crucial influence on the young man was a Quaker named Benjamin Lundy. While Beecher provided the religious philosophy that would be the basis for Garrison's opinions, Lundy supplied the cause he needed — antislavery.

Garrison met Lundy in 1828. At the time he had found work as the editor of a prohibition newspaper, the *National Philan-*

John
Greenleaf
Whittier

thropist. Along with his attacks on alcohol, he was busy writing biting editorials condemning gambling, prostitution, swearing, nonobservance of the Sabbath, and other forms of "immorality." Although he was aware of the slavery issue, he had not especially involved himself in it. Mildly interested in what Lundy had to say, he attended a lecture given by the Quaker to a group of Boston ministers.

As the lecture progressed, Garrison found himself listening with rapt attention. Benjamin Lundy, he discovered, was quite a man. Lundy had become a determined foe of slavery after a trip to Wheeling, Virginia, where he had seen slaves chained and marched through the streets on their way to the slave markets. Shortly afterward, at the age of twenty-six, he had organized the Union Humane Society in Saint Clairsville, Ohio, an antislavery organization whose membership quickly grew from five to five hundred. Six years later, he began an antislavery paper, the *Genius of Universal Emancipation,* which he published in Baltimore.

Garrison was inspired by Lundy's dedication and the facts the Quaker presented to back up his arguments for gradually abolishing slavery. From now on, Lundy's cause would be Garrison's cause. And from now on, that cause would never be the same. A little more than a year after meeting Lundy, Garrison accepted the older man's offer to join him in editing the *Genius of Universal Emancipation* in Baltimore.

By the time Garrison moved to Baltimore in September 1829, he had arrived at the basic principle that would guide all his antislavery work. This was a commitment to what he called "immediate and complete emancipation." It was a radical idea at a time when the most liberal whites spoke only of gradually abolishing slavery and allowing slaves time to become trained for their roles as freemen. Garrison was not the first person or the only one of his time to push "immediatism," but he was the most loud spoken. The term became his trademark, used again and again in speeches and editorials.

Garrison knew that Lundy took a much more conservative approach to emancipation and spoke in more muted terms than he. Before writing his first editorial for the *Genius,* he discussed their differences of opinion with his partner. "Well," Lundy told his brash young associate, "thee put thy initials to thy articles, and I will put my initials to mine, and each will bear his own burden."

Within a few months after joining the *Genius,* Garrison's "burden" led him to prison. In one of his editorials, he attacked a Newburyport merchant, Francis Todd, for carrying on the domestic slave trade. Todd didn't like Garrison's labeling him and the captain of his ship as "highway robbers and murderers" and "enemies of their own species." He promptly sued Garrison and Lundy for libel. A jury found Garrison guilty, as author of the article, and he was fined fifty dollars plus costs, which came to a total of about one hundred dollars. Because he had no money to pay the fine, Garrison had to accept a prison term of six months.

With a keen sense for public relations, Garrison saw the opportunities he could make of his jail term, and entered prison almost cheerfully. He wasted no time there. In a week he wrote *A Brief Sketch of the Trial of William Lloyd Garrison, for an alleged Libel of one Francis Todd, of Massachusetts,* in which he complained that his trial had been unfair and warned that he would not be silenced. Lundy distributed the pamphlet for him, reaching over a hundred newspapers and periodicals.

Before Garrison could serve out his sentence, his fine was paid and he was released. Arthur Tappan, his rescuer, was a wealthy New York businessman who would soon play an important part in the antislavery movement himself. Impressed with Garrison's pamphlet, Tappan paid his fine and sent him another hundred dollars to help in his work. Tappan's generosity did not end there. When Garrison wrote the philanthropist about his desire to publish an antislavery newspaper of his own, Tappan immediately sent a check, along with words of encouragement.

Delighted with Tappan's support, Garrison set out to raise additional money to begin a newspaper. As a fund-raising technique, he gave a series of antislavery lectures in the East. The highlight of his tour was a meeting in Boston on the evening of October 15, 1830. The audience he addressed that night included men who would become lifelong followers and devoted abolitionists. Among them were Samuel Joseph May, a Unitarian minister from Connecticut; his cousin, Samuel Sewall, a Boston lawyer and a descendant of Judge Samuel Sewall who had written *The Selling of Joseph;* and May's brother-in-law, Bronson Alcott, who later became a respected Boston lecturer and reformer. The angry style, the harsh language, the biting criticism that would characterize Garrison's antislavery attacks for years to come burst out in full flower at this lecture. His listeners were overwhelmed. "That is a providential man!" May told the others. "He is a prophet; he will shake our nation to its center, but he will shake slavery out of it."

The one person in the audience not impressed was Lyman

Beecher. The minister approached Garrison afterward and warned him that his zeal was "misguided," and that he ought to tone down his cry for immediate abolition. Garrison didn't answer, but his hero worship of Beecher had come to an end.

After the lecture, Alcott invited Garrison and some of his admirers to his home. Even while they congratulated the young lecturer, the men advised him to soften his language. May pleaded with him: ". . . do try to moderate your indignation, and keep more cool! why, you are all on fire." To which Garrison replied, "I have need to be all on fire, for I have mountains of ice about me to melt."

The time had come to lunge toward those mountains. Garrison decided to publish his new paper in Boston and to call it the *Liberator*. Isaac Knapp, a friend from Newburyport, joined him as a partner, and with the help of Sewall and May, 400 copies of the *Liberator* appeared on January 1, 1831. They were printed with borrowed type, but nothing else about them was borrowed. Here was William Lloyd Garrison's statement of intention. Here, printed in small type in four columns on the front page, was his famous editorial with his declaration of war and his promise to be *heard*.

Almost all the subscribers to the first issue of Garrison's paper were free blacks. Black leaders had come to know and admire him during his days on the *Genius*, when he showed growing sympathy for their cause. They had never met a white man quite like him. He seemed to understand their needs, to think the way they did, and to respect them without looking down on them. For his part, Garrison had felt a growing closeness to blacks that came from within him rather than from anything in his past. As he became more involved in antislavery, he turned more and more to the free black community for information and support. He often visited the homes of black leaders and invited them to his home, an unusual practice for even the most dedicated antislavery worker.

When Garrison announced his intention of starting the *Liberator*, blacks rallied to his side. On the day before the first issue was to appear, a wealthy black, James Forten, sent him the then large sum of fifty-four dollars, enough to cover the cost of twenty-seven subscriptions. Later, Forten bought more subscriptions for another twenty dollars. John B. Vashon, a Philadelphia barber, continually sent Garrison contributions to keep the paper going, allowing the editor to consider the money as loans. Even after three years of publishing, in 1834, about 1800 of the paper's 2300 subscribers were black.

The support of blacks pleased Garrison, but it was hardly enough to spread his ideas. For that he had another method, in which he used Southerners — his archenemies — as his springboard to fame. In Garrison's day, there were no wire services to supply newspapers with reports of events in different places. Instead, papers had a system of exchanges, in which they gathered information by sending one another copies of their publications. Garrison sent his newspaper to dozens of Southern editors. Shocked by his language and ideas, they printed blazing editorials that held him up as an example of Northern hatred and betrayal of the South. Their editorials always included long quotes from this "madman" whom they were growing to fear and despise. Northern editors picked up these quotes along with Southern comments to use in their papers because the controversy made good reading. Garrison, in turn, reprinted his original piece, Southern comments, Northern comments, and his own comments on what had been said. And that started everything going around again.

Within a few months after the first issue of the *Liberator* appeared Garrison's name was a household word throughout the country, while he and his partner were barely surviving on cakes and fruits sold in a basement shop of their office building. Many whites believed that the editor of the *Liberator* was a free black who should never have been freed; others maintained that he was a secret agent bent on stirring the South's slaves to rebellion.

The panic and anger that swept Southern states after Walker's *Appeal* and Nat Turner's revolt led to cries of revenge against Garrison and his antislavery paper. A vigilance committee in Columbia, South Carolina, offered a reward of $1500 for the capture of anyone found distributing the *Liberator*. The Georgia state legislature advertised a $5000 reward to anyone who would arrest Garrison and have him brought to Georgia for prosecution.

Actually, Garrison had condemned both Walker's call to revolt and Turner's upheaval. Although he used violent, revolutionary language, he opposed physical violence of any sort, and throughout his life remained a pacifist on issues that involved fighting or wars.

Unconcerned about the price on his head, Garrison busied himself planning an antislavery society in Boston. He hoped to make it the base for a network of new, militant societies throughout the country. Under his leadership, the New England Anti-Slavery Society was formed in January 1832. Twelve men, including Garrison, signed the preamble to the society's constitution. Garrison liked to compare them to the twelve Apostles of Christ going out to spread the word.

Now Garrison turned to another project that had been growing in his mind, debunking the American Colonization Society. In 1832, he published a thick pamphlet with an impossibly long title: *Thoughts on African Colonization: or an impartial exhibition of the doctrines, principles, and purposes of the American Colonization Society, together with the resolutions, addresses, and remonstrances of the free people of color.*

There was nothing "impartial" about the pamphlet. It attacked the Colonization Society and the people connected with it and made use of the name-calling for which Garrison was becoming known. A good part of the pamphlet was devoted to quotations from free blacks showing their strong objections to colonization.

The pamphlet was wordy and overdramatic. It included insults and half-truths stretched to make a point. Yet for all its faults, it represented a milestone in the antislavery struggle. It cried out for those basics of democracy upon which the nation had been founded. It presented the idea of slavery as a national sin that needed to be wiped away before any individual could consider himself a true Christian. This idea would be stressed again and again by abolitionists as the years went on. Perhaps most important, Garrison's *Thoughts on African Colonization* emphasized the equality of black people and condemned those who argued that the two races could not live and mingle freely with one another. Garrison was one of the few persons of his time to believe that blacks and whites were equals, socially, intellectually, and physically, and the only one to speak out so forcefully on the subject.

Garrison's pamphlet lost him many subscribers to the *Liberator*. But it also won influential reformers to the cause. Arthur Tappan bought and sent one hundred copies around to friends. Other antislavery sympathizers carefully weighed Garrison's arguments and finally broke with the Colonization Society. The arrogant, young, uncultured upstart from Newburyport effectively destroyed the influence of an organization that had absorbed much sincere antislavery energy in the country. The society would continue in existence for several more years, but altogether it could count only about 12,000 blacks that it had settled in Liberia.

To strengthen his position, Garrison took off for England in May 1833. His official reason was to raise money for a black school sponsored by the New England Society. His real reason was to thwart the efforts of one Elliott Cresson, who was trying to gather funds for the American Colonization Society in England. Garrison also wanted to know and become known by British abolitionists, who had accomplished in their country much of what he was struggling to gain in his.

The visit was a huge success. Garrison met major British abolitionists whose names had become honored among American antislavery workers. The young editor impressed the British with his sincerity and forcefulness. By the time he left, he had established himself in Britain as the leading American abolitionist. He returned home in September 1833, buoyed by the testimonials of British support he carried with him along with a protest from British leaders against the American Colonization Society.

The time had come now for Garrison to give up his one-man crusade and to join hands with other men and women who, more circumspectly and more quietly than he, also were promoting the abolition of slavery in the United States. The alliance would prove an uneasy one.

★ CHAPTER 5 ★

Abolitionists Unite

The object of this Society is the entire abolition of slavery in the United States . . . It shall aim to convince all our fellow-citizens, by arguments addresed to their understandings and consciences, that slave-holding is a heinous crime in the sight of God, and that the duty, safety, and best interests of all concerned, require its *immediate abandonment,* without expatriation . . . This society shall aim to elevate the character and conditions of the people of color, by encouraging their intellectual, moral, and religious improvement, and by removing public prejudice . . .

— Constitution of the American
Anti-Slavery Society, 1833

The brothers Arthur and Lewis Tappan took up antislavery as part of their determination to perfect the world. The brothers had made a fortune in silk trading and other business enterprises, and had become recognized as among the wealthiest businessmen in New York City. Then they had met Charles Grandison Finney and had set out on their religious mission to change society.

Finney was an evangelist, one of the most dynamic preachers of a religious revival — the Great Revival — which had rolled across the land. Finney preached that man had a choice in life. By choosing to repent from sin, a person could change his

The Tappan brothers, Lewis (left) and Arthur (right)

life and the lives of those around him. Five years before the Tappans met him, Finney had traveled through eastern New York State, holding revival meetings and inspiring listeners to a life of good works. He had been so effective that the region around Rochester got the nickname the "burned-over district" —burned by the flaming zeal of religion and good works. When Finney carried his fiery preachings to New York City, the Tappans, too, were caught up with his ideals of goodness and perfectionism.

With the money they had made, the Tappans went about the business of rehabilitating society. They opened churches for poor people in New York City and established one large church, the Chatham Street Chapel, in the downtown area, as a haven for anyone who wanted to use it. They hired the great Finney to serve as pastor of the church. To promote his views, they founded a weekly called the *New York Evangelist*. In his enthusiasm for reform, Arthur Tappan even sponsored an "Asylum for Females Who Have Deviated from the Paths of Virtue." It became one of his more ambitious failures.

It was natural that the Tappans' commitment to reform would lead them to the cause of the slave. They were not alone in their mission. The Great Revival and with it an increased desire to live by the principles of Christianity were motivating other liberal-minded whites to take up the fight against slavery. During the years in which Garrison was making his name known, other men and women in various parts of the country also were beginning to organize to oppose slavery more militantly than ever before.

In 1831, the year in which Garrison began his *Liberator*, the Tappans and other New York reformers organized a committee to discuss the idea of starting a national antislavery society. The early, moderate antislavery groups had established a loosely organized national society, but, like the state and local societies, it was so mild and soft spoken in its approach that it had made little impact. Many of the reformers who met with the Tappans had originally come from New England. Most knew little about Garrison. Some knew that his language and ideas were too extreme for them and they hoped to keep him out of any organization they founded.

One of the former New Englanders who would become a major voice in American abolition was a tall man with a twisted nose and heavy eyebrows that made him look as though he were always angry. Theodore Dwight Weld had a face that frightened children, but he had a way of talking in deep, resounding tones that gripped his listeners. Weld was born in

Connecticut. As a student, he became entranced with Finney's preachings, and, like the Tappans, was converted to the evangelist crusade of usefulness and good works. A British abolitionist had interested him in the antislavery cause, which now occupied his attention more and more.

Other members of the New York Committee included Joshua Leavitt, a New England lawyer and preacher who had come to New York to edit the Tappan's paper, the *Evangelist*; Simeon Jocelyn, a white minister who headed a black congregation in New Haven and was devoted to founding a black college in New Haven; William Goodell, who had taken over the *National Philanthropist* after Garrison left and now edited other reform papers; and William Jay, son of John Jay, the first chief justice of the United States Supreme Court. All of them were distinguished men. Each was devoted to various reforms other than slavery, and each hoped to change the world a little by changing the evil he saw about him.

The committee organized in 1831 decided that the time was not yet ripe for a national antislavery society, but much could be done to prepare the way. Shortly after this meeting, Weld set out on a lecture tour of the West and South. His purpose was to raise funds and to find a location for a theological seminary, sponsored by the Tappans, that would train preachers in Finney's methods. During his travels, he held serious soul-searching discussions about slavery with various groups that he met. One of the most far-reaching of these talks took place in Huntsville, Alabama. Here Weld met James G. Birney, a prosperous young lawyer and planter and a slaveholder with a troubled conscience. As a result of the meeting, Birney gave up both his slaves and his legal practice to begin a career in the antislavery cause. That career and that cause would lead him to seek the Presidency of the United States one day.

In the course of his tour, Weld visited Western Reserve College in Hudson, Ohio. Unlike the more conservative schools of the East, colleges in the West reflected the freewheeling openness and emphasis on the individual typical of the frontier. At Western Reserve and other Western schools, students and faculty were discussing the slavery issue and seeking solutions to it. Soon, the Western colleges would become well-springs of abolition and focal points of a campus unrest uncommon in the more established universities and colleges of the East.

Weld met the president of Western Reserve, Charles B. Storrs, and several faculty members. One of them, Beriah Green, had read Garrison's *Thoughts on Colonization*, and immediately turned against the American Colonization Society. He and a young professor of mathematics, Elizur Wright, Jr., influenced other faculty members to take a firm stand against colonization. Shortly after Weld's visit Wright left the college for New York to serve as secretary of the Tappans' New York Committee. When Weld visited them, the men at Western Reserve were talking about forming a national antislavery society along the same lines as the New York group. Weld departed knowing that his New York friends would have strong support from these dedicated men in the West.

After much searching, in the spring of 1832, Weld could report to the Tappans that he had fulfilled his mission. In Cincinnati, he discovered a small, struggling theological school that seemed just the right training ground for an army of

Finney evangelists. Lane Seminary had been started by a group of clergymen and was attracting students with antislavery leanings who had been forced to flee the South. The Tappans agreed to take over and appointed Lyman Beecher to head their new institution. Weld, who knew many Finney converts, helped gather a group of brilliant students.

Meanwhile, the New York reformers grew more committed than ever to creating a national society. At this point, Garrison entered the scene. Back from his triumphant tour of England, he heard about the committee's plans, and urged that a national convention be called immediately. Garrison had had little to do with the committee. But, for now, his prestige among British abolitionists enhanced his influence over Americans. Although the New Yorkers wanted more time to plan their convention, they agreed to call it for December 4, 1833, in Philadelphia.

The turnout was disappointing on that cold December day when delegates from New York, Boston, Pennsylvania, and Ohio met to form a national abolitionist organization, the American Anti-Slavery Society. About sixty antislavery representatives appeared. Lewis Tappan came, along with Elizur Wright and Beriah Green, who was elected president of the convention. Garrison came with members of the New England Anti-Slavery Society. Four women attended the meeting, an unusual occurrence during an age when women were supposed to be home cooking or tending to their children and not taking part in conventions, much less radical conventions.

Early on, Lewis Tappan warned other delegates that Garrison's name should not be "inserted prominently" in the proceedings because it might "keep away many professed friends of abolition." As much as they could, the delegates tried to keep

Garrison in the background. They gave him the relatively un-
important position of secretary of foreign correspondence, and
they elected Arthur Tappan president of the new society and
Lewis Tappan a member of the executive committee. The
convention did not even place Garrison on the committee that
drew up its constitution. But the constitution the committee
prepared included principles Garrison had stated many times,
including a demand for immediate emancipation.

"The object of this Society," declared the constitution, "is
the entire abolition of slavery in the United States . . ." Laced
throughout the constitution and other writings of the convention was an emphasis on "moral suasion," by which the abolitionists would appeal to the consciences and moral beliefs of
their countrymen in trying to persuade them to end slavery
immediately.

As a gesture to Garrison's achievements, the convention delegates did allow him to draw up their Declaration of Sentiments.
In it he pointed out that fifty-seven years had passed since
another convention had met in the same city of Philadelphia
to prepare another declaration, the Declaration of Independence. In view of the principles of that declaration, he wrote,
America's "guilt of oppression is unequalled by any other on
the face of the earth." Again and again over the years, Garrison
and other abolitionists would remind Americans of the gap
that existed between their ideals as stated in the Declaration of
Independence and their practices.

Soon after the convention, the society established its headquarters in New York, where Arthur Tappan pumped funds
into the treasury to keep the shaky organization on its feet. It
published a newspaper, the *Emancipator*, along with dozens of

EMANCIPATOR—*EXTRA.*

NEW-YORK, SEPTEMBER 2, 1839.

American Anti-Slavery Almanac for 1840.

The seven cuts following, are selected from thirteen, which may be found in the Anti-slavery Almanac for 1840. They represent well-authenticated facts, and illustrate in various ways, the cruelties daily inflicted upon three millions of native born Americans, by their low-countrymen! A brief explanation follows each cut.

The peculiar " Domestic Institutions of our Southern brethren."

Illustrated front page of the *Emancipator*

antislavery pamphlets. And it appointed agents to carry its antislavery message to the public. The agents received a weekly salary of eight dollars for lecturing and helping to organize local antislavery societies.

Throughout the first months of its existence the American Anti-Slavery Society struggled along with few members. Many of the country's leading citizens and thousands of others who opposed slavery refused to join abolitionist organizations, which they felt were building up differences between the North and the South and splitting the nation. But by the end of the 1830s, the ranks of the national society had swelled to include about 250,000 members in 1350 state and local chapters.

A campus rebellion gave the society the push it needed to grow in strength. Theodore Weld had turned Lane Seminary in Cincinnati into a center of abolitionist thought. Early in 1834, he organized a debate on slavery among the students and faculty. Almost everyone at the institution became caught up in this Lane Debate. After nine exhausting days of discussion, the students and some of their professors took a stand in favor of immediate abolition and against colonization. They also set up their own antislavery society and began a program of helping blacks in the community.

The Lane Debate led to open warfare between the conservative board of trustees and the radical antislavery students and professors. The board broke up the antislavery society and forbade extracurricular activities in behalf of blacks. President Lyman Beecher, always wavering between moral indignation at slavery and disapproval of the methods of abolitionists, backed the trustees.

The turmoil at Lane had repercussions in other parts of the country. Representatives of a number of universities met to review the turn of events there. As a result of this meeting, such colleges as Harvard, Yale, and Princeton issued rules forbidding their students to organize antislavery societies or even to discuss the subject. Although a few students defied the orders, most accepted them without struggle. Even when antislavery grew and spread, it did not become a major issue on America's most prestigious campuses.

The Lane rebels would not give in so easily. In anger at Beecher and the board of trustees, forty students, including Weld, resigned from the seminary. It did not take long for them to find another home. Oberlin College, in northeastern Ohio, had been opened in 1833 as a liberal, coeducational school and by 1834 was in financial trouble. With a guarantee that the institution would take an antislavery stand and also admit blacks, Arthur Tappan agreed to put up the money to begin a theology department there. Weld and the other Lane-rebels entered Oberlin and soon made it a new base for abolitionist activity in the West.

As a way to help promote the American Anti-Slavery Society, Weld chose seventy Oberlin students to become agents of the society. He trained them so carefully that they became the organization's best agents. Each would-be agent went through an exacting course in which he reviewed all the antislavery arguments and rehearsed answers to dozens of proslavery statements. Many of the young men had been converts of Finney, familiar with the emotional techniques the evangelist used to bring his audience to Christ. Now they fanned out across the country in a crusade to use those techniques in the antislavery cause, turning abolition into an evangelical mission against sin.

★ CHAPTER 6 ★

New England — Hotbed of Abolition

THOMPSON
THE ABOLITIONIST!!!!!
That infamous foreign scoundrel Thompson will hold forth
this afternoon, at the Liberator Office No. 48 Washington
Street. The present is a fair opportunity for the friends of
the Union to *snake Thompson out!* It will be a contest between the Abolitionists and the friends of the Union. A
purse of $100 has been raised by a number of patriotic citi-
zens to reward the individual who shall first lay violent
hands on Thompson, so that he may be brought to the tar-
kettle before dark. Friends of the Union, be vigilant!
Boston, Wednesday, 12 o'clock
— Anonymous handbill, 1835

It was October 21, 1835, and the ladies of the Boston Female
Anti-Slavery Society had scheduled a meeting. The women
had invited William Lloyd Garrison and the British abolitionist
George Thompson to address their meeting. The invitation to
Thompson had gone out in spite of the fact that he had caused
a furor with a series of antislavery lectures he had given in
various Northern states. Newspapers had expressed their anger
at having a foreigner come to their country and self-righteously
tell Americans how to change their society. Some of the people
had expressed themselves more directly, by hurling garbage at

the lecturer. This very morning in Boston, two merchants had printed and distributed handbills that called on Bostonians to take measures to *"snake Thompson out!"*

The ladies were not put off by the anger and threats against Thompson. Nor were they frightened by the increasingly hostile attitude people were taking toward the abolitionists. Like their menfolk, they chose to believe that the strong reactions abolitionists had aroused recently proved that they were making an impression on their countrymen.

The day dawned clear and calm, the kind of fine fall day that Bostonians don't often enjoy. But the air crackled with electricity as a tense city waited for the meeting. A mob of more than 200 people gathered around the antislavery headquarters on Washington Street, waiting for the hated Thompson to arrive. Inside, about twenty-five women waited too, patiently, showing no signs of the anxiety most of them felt. About two thirty, Garrison arrived and elbowed his way through the mob to the ladies' meeting hall. Thompson, it turned out, would not be present.

In fact, he had left town. Garrison tried to convince a crowd of men who had shoved their way in to leave but succeeded only in infuriating them. Amidst shouts and shaking fists, Boston's Mayor Theodore Lyman arrived to plead with the ladies to disband their meeting and go home. After some protests the women voted to adjourn. Silently they filed out of the building, past the screaming mob, which had now doubled in number.

Left without a meeting and under siege by a mob that had torn down the antislavery sign outside and was now crying for his head, Garrison decided to escape by a back window. From the window he crawled into a nearby carpenter's shop, where he hid behind a pile of boards. The trick failed. Within seconds the mob spotted him, tied a rope around him, and dragged him out into the street.

"Kill him!" "Lynch him!" "Hang the abolitionist!" people shouted. Later, a member of the mob told Garrison that the plan was "to take you and Mr. Thompson to the Common,

William Lloyd Garrison has a narrow escape from an angry crowd

strip, tar-and-feather you, and then dye your face and hands black in a manner that would never change from a night negro color."

Luckily for Garrison, the plan was stopped. Two strong men seized the abolitionist and ushered him through the crowd to City Hall. "He shan't be hurt," one of them shouted at the frenzied mob. "You shan't hurt him. He's an American." Some people around picked up the cry and helped move Garrison to safety. Inside City Hall the shouts of the angry rioters could still be heard, and the mayor decided to lock Garrison in jail overnight to protect him. In typical Garrison fashion, the abolitionist explained later that he retired to his cell "accompanied by two delightful associates — a good conscience and a cheerful mind." He was freed on condition that he leave town for a while, which he did.

From the window of his law office, Wendell Phillips saw it all. It was a new office, opened a short time before, after Phillips had graduated from Harvard Law School. The beginning lawyer had plenty of time to look out the window; he could count on his fingers the number of clients he had. But then, Wendell Phillips really did not have to worry about earning a living. He came from one of the wealthiest and most distinguished families of Boston. His father, John Phillips, had been the city's first mayor, conservative and highly respected. Many of his ancestors had been judges and governors. Wendell had grown up in a big mansion in the upper-crust Beacon Hill section of Boston. At Harvard College, which he attended before law school, he became known as the "pet of the aristocracy." Tall and thin, with fine regular features, he was in every sense the aristocrat, the Boston Brahmin. (The name, based on the Brahmans who made up India's highest caste, was coming into vogue to stand for Boston's first families.) Phillips seemed the last person in the world to ever become involved with "crazy" Garrison and his "infamous" paper.

Phillips stood at the window and watched for a while. Then he went down to the street to see what the commotion was all about. As he worked his way through the crowd, he noticed in amazement that many of his friends and associates from Beacon Hill were among the rioters. Later, this crowd would become known as the "broadcloth mob." Well-dressed, with kid gloves and broadcloth coats, they were mostly "gentlemen of property and standing" who had made a great deal of money as merchants and shippers, and who had strong business ties to the South. Only a few weeks earlier, a Virginia newspaper had written a warning about the abolitionists that these Boston businessmen took to heart: "The people of the North must go to hanging these fanatical wretches if they would not lose the benefit of the Southern trade; and they *will* do it. They know too well which side their bread is buttered on, ever to give up these advantages." The men Phillips saw about him knew which side their bread was buttered on. They wanted to stop the abolitionists before it was too late.

Wendell Phillips looked at the pushing, shoving, shouting men whose faces were twisted with hatred. They belonged to his world. He had far more in common with them than with any Garrison or Theodore Weld. But now he stood among them as though they were strangers. "I hope they tar and feather him," he heard a justice of the peace say of Garrison.

"Though I would not assist, I can tell them five dollars are ready for the man that will do it." Phillips stared at him in horror.

Few people can point to a moment in time and say, "that was a turning point in my life." Wendell Phillips could. The scene he witnessed on Boston's cobblestone streets set him on a new course in life. As a wealthy young man beginning a new law practice, he had felt an emptiness, a need to give meaning to a life of ease. Now he found that meaning.

Not long after the broadcloth mob scene, Phillips met the beautiful Ann Terry Greene and quickly fell in love. From a well-to-do family herself, Miss Greene had been orphaned at a young age and reared by close friends of Garrison, Henry and Maria Chapman. Through her, Phillips met Garrison and

Wendell Phillips

other abolitionists. Shortly after his marriage to Ann, Phillips openly joined the abolitionist movement. On June 14, 1837, he made his maiden speech before an antislavery convention in Lynn, Massachusetts. Although many of Phillips' staid Boston friends had heard him speak with growing sympathy of the abolitionists, his outright conversion to their cause stunned Beacon Hill. He was branded a "friend of the niggers" and a "madman." Clients kept away from his shiny law office, and acquaintances refused to speak to him when they met him on the street. Some relatives even tried to have him declared insane and sent to a mental institution.

Phillips never wavered from the cause. He became its most eloquent spokesman and one of the great speakers of the period. Unlike Garrison and other abolitionists, he did not fill his speeches with pompous phrases, nor use exaggerated gestures to make his points. He spoke in a conversational tone, relaxed, easy, always in complete control of himself. People who heard him speak called him the "golden trumpet" of the abolitionists.

For more than thirty years, Phillips served as a loyal follower of Garrison. He stood by Garrison's most radical doctrines and defended his chief even when other friends turned against him. When the Civil War ended, however, he, too, finally broke with the old man.

The broadcloth mob was the moving force behind Phillips' conversion to abolition. But Phillips was not alone among Boston's finest in dedicating himself to the abolitionist crusade. As the 1830s moved along, New England began to emerge as a center for the most radical and outspoken abolitionist activities in the country. Influenced by Garrison, New Englanders from many walks of life joined the cause, willingly throwing their good names and positions into the fight against slavery. At first, most of these New Englanders accepted Garrison's creeds and leadership and became known as the "Garrisonians" among other abolitionists. Like Phillips, however, a good many of them split with him as time went on.

Samuel May and Samuel Sewall, among the first of Garrison's followers, both came from prominent families. May, a Harvard graduate, was a young minister in a well-endowed Connecticut parish. Sewall, a descendant of Judge Samuel Sewall, was himself a highly successful lawyer. Another proper Bostonian lawyer, Ellis Gray Loring, became a Garrison supporter shortly after May and Sewall. He was perhaps the first white lawyer to train a black man for the bar by having the man work in his law office — a system disapproved of by whites, who found it difficult to accept blacks in professional positions.

Francis Jackson turned to abolitionism on the day he saw his fellow Bostonians mob Garrison. A rich, conservative businessman, Jackson felt so shaken by the actions of his associates that he invited the members of the Boston Female Anti-Slavery Society to use his home for their next meeting. They did, fearful throughout that the house might be invaded or burned. Later, Jackson served as president of the Massachusetts Anti-Slavery Society (the name taken by the New England society after a few years).

Edmund Quincy, son of Harvard's president Josiah Quincy and a friend of Wendell Phillips', joined the movement two years after Phillips did. This betrayal turned his aristocratic friends against him and made him the target of vicious rumors. His enemies called him "His Anti-Slavery Highness" and accused him of beating his wife and bringing black women into his home to live with him.

After Dr. Henry Bowditch became an open abolitionist, he found the doors of prestigious Massachusetts General Hospital closed to him. Heir to a respected Boston family, Bowditch had been offered a position as admitting physician on the hospital staff before his "disgraceful" affiliation with the abolitionists. The physician made a point of getting to know free blacks and entertaining them in his home, a practice guaranteed to alienate his neighbors.

Charles T. Follen also sacrificed his career for the cause he came to believe in. A refugee from Austria, where he had opposed the rule of Napoleon Bonaparte, Follen was a professor of German language and literature at Harvard until he joined the New England Anti-Slavery Society in 1834. The next year he lost his job, although he was far more soft spoken and moderate in his approach than Garrison and some of the others. Follen died tragically in 1840 when the steamer *Lexington* sank on Long Island Sound. The Unitarian church with which he had been associated refused to hold services for him because of his abolitionist activities.

"The cause is worthy of Gabriel — yea, the God of Hosts places Himself at its head. Whittier, enlist! . . ." With these words, Garrison lured his early protégé, poet John Greenleaf Whittier, into the antislavery campaign, and Whittier came wholeheartedly. In 1833, he wrote a pamphlet called *Justice and Expediency* in which he gave reasons for the necessity of immediate emancipation. He published 500 copies of it at his own expense. Later, Arthur Tappan reprinted it, circulating 5000 copies. It became one of the important abolitionist papers.

Many of Whittier's poems, such as "The Slave Ships," portrayed the wrongs of slavery in strong, emotional language.

Another New England poet, James Russell Lowell, joined the movement not because of Garrison but because of his bride, Maria White, who was a confirmed abolitionist. He became a faithful supporter of Garrison and an active member of the Massachusetts Anti-Slavery Society. Although he did not want to be paid for his antislavery writings, Lowell finally agreed to accept $500 a year to write for the *Anti-Slavery Standard* because his abolitionist works prevented other pieces from being accepted by literary journals.

There were other New England abolitionists, some so inspired by their chosen cause that they outdid even Garrison in

James
Russell
Lowell

extremism. Among them were Stephen Foster and Parker Pillsbury. These two radicals made the churches of New England their special targets of attack. During the late 1830s many churches refused to permit the abolitionists to use their chapels to deliver lectures, as they had been doing. The two men would plant themselves in the front pews of a church on a Sunday morning. Just as the sermon was about to begin, one of them would rise and ask to speak in the name of the suffering slave. Usually, before they could plead their case, they would be tossed out. Foster once had his collarbone broken in being thrown to the street, but he went right on invading churches as soon as he was well. Foster married one of the most outspoken women abolitionists, Abby Kelley, and the two combined efforts to fight for emancipation, women's rights, and other reforms.

With these antislavery fighters and others less known, New England remained a hotbed of abolition until the Civil War ended slavery. There were a variety of reasons why the antislavery movement had such a stronghold in New England. On a superficial level, New Englanders found it easy to become morally indignant about a situation that existed hundreds of miles away from them. They did not have to worry about facing the rehabilitation of millions of freed slaves, nor did they have to consider living among a black population that would outnumber them. They could dedicate themselves to the black cause and cry out for reform in the South while closing their eyes to other problems that existed around them, such as the poor working conditions of white laborers in the North.

The spurt of antislavery activity in New England beginning in the 1830s may also have involved something of a class struggle. Many of the antislavery devotees were professional people from good, stolid New England families. Some were aristocrats, from the wealthiest and most elite backgrounds. Very few were merchants or manufacturers. The merchant group had grown rich and powerful during the 1800s through shipbuilding, slave trading, and cotton manufacturing. Bit by bit the newly rich businessmen had climbed New England's social ladder to push aside the older, long-time upper classes. By opposing slavery, professional people and aristocrats could fight the merchants who not only had profited from slavery but also had taken over their own places in society.

But New England's dedication to the struggle for liberty went deeper than these factors. At its root lay a love of freedom that was part of the New England heritage. Boston and other sections of New England had been the breeding place of the Revolutionary War. The spirit of that Revolution still lived on and was part of the people's lives. Many New Englanders spoke of the antislavery cause as the unfinished revolution. To complete the work their forefathers had begun, they felt they must bring freedom to the enslaved blacks.

And along with the old Revolutionary War ideals, there was a different kind of revolution in the air. People in Massachusetts, in Vermont, in many areas of New England were experimenting with new ways of thinking and new ways of living. Young people and old joined cooperative communities, such as George Ripley's Brook Farm, outside of Boston. Some, as members of John Humphrey Noyes' Oneida Community, tried out new forms of family life. That colony had a system of "complex marriage," in which men and women lived together freely with no marriage contracts and reared children as a community responsibility.

Most typical of the revolt of the spirit were the Transcendentalists. This group of intellectuals included such people as Ralph Waldo Emerson, Nathaniel Hawthorne, and Henry David Thoreau. Their revolt involved turning back to nature and away from the rigid institutions of society. They spoke of man's ability to transcend, or go beyond, the physical world to achieve the highest goals of which he is capable. The Transcendentalists despised slavery, yet most were too much the individualists to join an organized antislavery movement. Many, too, objected to the brutal language and radical actions of some of the abolitionists. Still, the spirit that moved the New England Transcendentalists — the belief in the individual and his abilities — was the same kind of spirit that moved the abolitionists. Throughout New England there was a surge of freedom; freedom for man as a whole among some thinkers, for the black man in particular among others.

★ CHAPTER 7 ★

Martyrs of the Movement

---

1. Abolitionists hold that "all men are born free and equal, endowed by their Creator with certain inalienable rights, among which are life, LIBERTY, and the pursuit of happiness." They do not believe that these rights are abrogated, or at all modified by the color of the skin ...

2. As the above-mentioned rights are in their nature inalienable, it is not possible that one man can convert another into a piece of property ...

3. Abolitionists, therefore, hold American slavery to be a *wrong,* a legalized system of inconceivable injustice, and a SIN ...

4. . . . . Abolitionists believe that all who hold slaves, or who approve the practice in others, should *immediately* cease to do so.

5. Lastly, Abolitionists believe that as all men are *born* free, so all who are now held as slaves in this country were BORN FREE, and that they are slaves now is the sin, not of those who introduced the race into this country, but of those, and those alone, who now hold them ...

— ELIJAH LOVEJOY, martyred abolitionist, in
the *Observer,* 1837

Elijah Lovejoy had come to the peaceful town of Alton, Illinois, in the summer of 1836. He moved there from St. Louis where he had made many enemies because of the antislavery views he expressed in his newspaper, the *Observer*. He had assured the citizens of Alton that although he opposed slavery, he was not an abolitionist bent on destroying the slave system. His paper, he said, was a religious one and his attitude toward slavery stemmed from Christian teachings. The people had believed him and accepted him as a man of principle. Their state did not permit slavery, and many of them disliked the slave system also. When ruffians dumped Lovejoy's printing press into the Mississippi River the day after he arrived, a group of Alton citizens banded together to buy him a new printing press, and pledged to defend freedom of the press.

During the year that he lived in Alton, Lovejoy gained more than 2000 subscribers to his paper. But he also went back on his word. Instead of limiting himself to religious topics, he turned more and more to the issue of slavery. Although he had not started out as an abolitionist, he found himself increasingly caught up in the antislavery movement. In one editorial after another, he attacked slaveholders and called for an end to all slavery in the United States. He even helped establish a state antislavery society and boldly printed in his paper the principles that guided abolitionists.

The citizens of Alton began to worry about Mr. Lovejoy. Located near the mouths of the Missouri and Illinois rivers, their city was a bustling port, trading with Southern as well as Northern cities. Lovejoy's continuing attacks on slavery endangered their trade with the South, a major source of their income.

Almost overnight, people who had at first welcomed the editor turned against him. On his way home from work one evening a group of men rushed him and threatened to tar and feather him if he did not stop his troublemaking. Another time a mob broke into the warehouse where he kept his printing press and dumped it into the Mississippi River. When Lovejoy bought a new press, a mob destroyed it, too. Finally, the townspeople held a public meeting protesting Lovejoy's antislavery writings and resolving that he must leave town. Had he left quietly, the whole matter would have died down. Instead, he went before the townspeople and stated his position. He spoke of freedom of the press and his right to express his views. He ended with a refusal to compromise.

". . . I have concluded, after consultation with my friends, and earnestly seeking counsel of God," Lovejoy told the people of Alton, "to remain at Alton and here to insist on protection in the exercise of my rights. If the civil authorities refuse to protect me, I must look to God, and if I die, I have determined to make my grave in Alton."

Then he and his supporters made plans to get another new press to replace the last one destroyed, and to continue the paper just as it had been before. They also prepared to defend the press once they got it. Some of the men who joined Lovejoy in his stand had little feeling for the antislavery cause. But they believed strongly in freedom of the press and the protection of property, and they were willing to fight for those beliefs.

Everybody in Alton knew when the new press arrived — on November seventh at three o'clock in the morning. Townspeople blew horns and rang bells as Lovejoy and about thirty supporters carried it to the warehouse. Word spread that another thirty men joined the first group in the warehouse to help defend the press from attackers.

The day passed quietly, and by nine o'clock at night most of

Lovejoy's supporters returned home. Then, close to midnight, a noisy mob gathered outside the warehouse. Many of the men had been drinking heavily in waterfront bars. As time wore on, others joined them, including some of the most prominent citizens of the town.

In the midst of the noise and shouting, a group of attackers climbed to the roof of the building and set it afire. Lovejoy and two other men started out to stop the flames. Suddenly shots rang out. Lovejoy turned around quickly and ran back inside. "Oh God, I am shot, I am shot," he cried, as he fell to the ground. He was dead within moments.

The following day, Lovejoy's friends and relatives carried his body from the warehouse to a funeral home. "If I only had a fife, I would play the Dead March for him," jeered one of the leaders of the mob that had murdered him. As the victim's body lay in its simple pine box, his younger brother Owen vowed before it that he would never give up the fight against slavery. Later, Owen Lovejoy would become a powerful anti-slavery congressman from Illinois. On November 9, 1837, Elijah Lovejoy was buried in the midst of a pouring rain with little ceremony. That day would have been his thirty-fifth birthday.

Elijah Lovejoy was the first martyr of the abolition movement. His death, wrote former President John Quincy Adams, caused "a shock as of an earthquake throughout this continent." The murder became a symbol of the divisions that would soon rip the nation apart. And it served as a forecast of the violence that would grow and spread during the next two decades until it would explode in bloody civil war.

Everywhere in the North, men and women gathered to hold

The Alton riot where Elijah Lovejoy was killed by a mob incensed over his antislavery editorials

protest meetings in honor of the dead man. At a huge public meeting in Boston's Faneuil Hall, Wendell Phillips burst into an unprepared speech in defense of Lovejoy, marking his debut as one of the giants of the abolition movement and one of the great orators of his time. And at a quiet memorial meeting in Ohio, another young man raised his right hand and swore to devote his life to the destruction of slavery. He was John Brown. In years to come he would join Elijah Lovejoy in martyrdom.

Ironically, many abolitionists did not wholly admire Lovejoy or sympathize with the way in which he died, although few said so publicly. They objected to the fact that Lovejoy had taken up arms to defend his press. Like Garrison, most abolitionists were pacifists at this time and were determined to fight the antislavery battle without resorting to violence.

But violence was everywhere in those years. While the abolitionists tried to avoid it, their opponents did not. The broadcloth mob's attack on Garrison and the murder of Lovejoy were part of a series of violent incidents that now began to plague the abolitionists.

Amos Dresser had headed South to sell Bibles and other books, hoping to earn extra money to support himself through Lane Seminary. He took along some antislavery papers and pamphlets, to read on the trip, he said later. The young theology student got as far as Nashville, Tennessee. There he was arrested and accused of being "very hostile to slavery." Although he had broken no law, a vigilance committee made up of leading citizens and clergymen found him guilty on three counts: being a member of an antislavery society in another state, having antislavery literature in his possession, and being suspected of distributing that literature. They set his punishment at twenty lashes to be beaten on his bare back.

At the marketplace, young Dresser was stripped before a jeering, laughing crowd. While church bells chimed, he was whipped and then ordered to leave town. "He should have been hung up as high as Haman to rot upon the gibbet until the wind whipped through his bones," a Georgia newspaper wrote. "The cry of the whole South should be Death, Instant Death, to the Abolitionist, whenever he is caught."

Marius Robinson, one of Theodore Weld's followers, gave an antislavery lecture in Berlin, Ohio. The next day he was kidnaped, tarred and feathered, and dumped beside a roadside. He never completely recovered from the experience for the rest of his life.

A college student named Samuel Hall began speaking about

abolition to an audience in Marietta, Ohio. Within minutes, he was pelted with rotten eggs and stormed by a mob. He had to swim across the Muskingum River to escape.

James G. Birney, the Southern slaveholder-turned-abolitionist, began a newspaper called the *Philanthropist* in Cincinnati to speak to Southerners about slavery. A short time later, his office was torn apart and his home wrecked. Constantly persecuted by mobs, Birney finally fled to New York, where he worked as secretary of the American Anti-Slavery Society.

The "Martyr Age" was the name the English writer Harriet Martineau gave the abolitionists of the 1830s. Mobs, rotten eggs, beatings, tar barrels, and jail terms became part of their daily lives as they stubbornly went about the country preaching their doctrine of freedom. The abolitionists hit the American people hard, and like wounded animals the people lunged back at them.

The abolitionist demand that created the greatest furor and aroused the most violent response was their insistence on immediate emancipation. All antislavery groups proclaimed this doctrine, but the different groups of abolitionists had different explanations for what they meant by "immediatism." To Garrison and his followers, immediate emancipation seemed to mean giving the slaves immediate freedom but, in some undefined way, supervising them and holding back many of their civil liberties until they became educated and ready. To New York abolitionists, it meant "immediate emancipation gradually accomplished." And that meant that the nation should decide immediately to free the slaves, but then free them only gradually after they had been prepared to take their places in society. Western abolitionists turned the New York slogan around to "gradual emancipation immediately begun" which was a plea for the immediate acceptance of the idea that slavery was a sin and then gradual abolition.

With all the twists and turns and plays on words, the public had a difficult time understanding the abolitionists' explanations. Northerners and Southerners saw only the specter of millions of uneducated slaves suddenly turned loose to wander about, perhaps robbing or even killing whites. And the abolitionists took no pains to ease those fears by spelling out a practical plan for how their immediate emancipation could be executed. They viewed themselves as agitators getting the public to face the slavery issue. They spoke in extreme terms in order to arouse the conscience of the nation. When people had determined to act on slavery, they said, then the details of policy and procedures for emancipation could be worked out.

What made the immediatist slogan especially hard for people to accept was the abolitionist demand that immediate emancipation was to be accomplished without compensation to slaveholders for their loss of human property. Since slavery was a sin, the abolitionists argued, it made no sense to pay people for ceasing to commit that sin. Again, the lack of a practical means for dealing with slaveholders made the abolitionist arguments seem meaningless to the general public.

Along with their doctrines of emancipation, the abolitionist emphasis on the equality of blacks angered whites. In defiance of accepted beliefs and traditions, the abolitionists proclaimed again and again that the black was the equal of the white man, and that given equal opportunities he could accomplish as much. By freeing the slaves and then educating them, the abolitionists said, Americans would improve their society.

To promote their ideas, the abolitionists used every propaganda technique they could muster, and these techniques, like the principles they advertised, irritated Americans. But they also kept the antislavery cause in the public's mind and on its conscience.

Abolitionist agents blanketed the North, East, and West, speaking in churches, halls, schoolhouses, and even stables. Proudly they paraded their torn clothes and battered hats to show their audiences what mobs had done to them. Abolitionist societies published thousands of antislavery essays and pamphlets. In the year 1837 alone, more than 50,000 abolitionist pamphlets and circulars appeared. More than forty periodicals and newspapers carried the antislavery message. Special periodicals for children printed poems and essays to turn young hearts to the cause. Typical was this verse from a children's ABC book:

> *A is an Abolitionist*
> *A man who wants to free*
> *The wretched slave, and give to all*
> *An equal liberty.*

Abolitionist books portrayed the life of the slave in great detail, giving special emphasis to cases of cruelty and separation of slave families. One of the most effective of these was Theodore Weld's book *Slavery As It Is,* published in 1839. To compile it, Weld, his wife, Angelina, and his sister-in-law Sarah Grimké poured over thousands of Southern newspapers — more than 20,000 by their own count. Based on ads in those papers for runaway slaves or slaves for sale, they drew up a dictionary of cruelties to slaves. An entry might be an ad in which an owner described a runaway with the words "I burnt her with a hot iron, on the left side of her face. I tried to make the letter 'M.'" Or it might tell of a missing slave who could be identified because he had "his left eye out." The book was a great success, selling more than 20,000 copies within four months. It became a gold mine of references for abolitionist lecturers and a source book for Harriet Beecher Stowe's *Uncle Tom's Cabin* a dozen years later.

In all the abolitionist writings and lectures the South came under fierce attack, and it was there that the antislavery workers aroused the greatest anger and hatred. Southerners believed that the abolitionists were deliberately trying to stir up slave rebellions. To stop them, laws were passed to prohibit anti-slavery societies in Southern states, and Southerners tried, in whatever ways they could, to keep antislavery pamphlets and other literature out of their states. In July 1835, a group of citizens of Charleston, South Carolina, broke into the town's post office, seized all literature that bore the name of an anti-slavery society, and publicly burned it. When abolitionists appealed to the United States postmaster general, Amos Kendall, they received no support. Kendall backed the Charleston postmaster, who approved of the burning.

President Andrew Jackson backed Kendall. Although an ardent advocate of democracy, Jackson was a Southerner and a slaveholder himself and he approached the slave situation from those points of view. It was natural for Jackson to dislike and distrust the abolitionists, the more so because most of them backed the Whig Party rather than his Democratic Party, and much of his own political support came from the South. He labeled abolitionist literature a "wicked plan of inciting Negroes to insurrection and massacre." In a message to Congress, he asked for a law to prohibit antislavery writings from the mails because they were "incendiary publications." The law was never passed.

In defending themselves against abolitionist attacks, Southerners took the position that slavery was a "positive good" that benefited all of society. The economic development of the South — and with it the North — they said, depended on slave labor. And the rules and regulations of slavery, along with the good example of white culture, were the only means of elevating the black people. They pointed out also that slavery had existed in Biblical times and been regulated by ancient law, so that "it was of God," as one Southerner explained. The governor of South Carolina summed up the feelings of slaveholders when he said, "In all social systems there must be a class to do the menial duties, to perform the drudgery of life . . ." The blacks provided the South with that class.

Northerners reacted to the abolitionists with almost as much fear and anger as the Southerners. Northern businessmen had a vested interest in keeping on good terms with the South. "Mr. May," a businessmen told Samuel May, "we are not such fools as not to know that slavery is a great evil, a great wrong." But, he went on, "we cannot afford, sir, to let you and your association succeed in your endeavor to overthrow slavery. It is not a matter of principle with us. It is a matter of business necessity . . ." This business necessity led otherwise staid and proper businessmen to take part in riots and physical attacks on the abolitionists as they made their way across the lecture trails.

Many Northerners did not like slavery any more than the abolitionists did, and they hoped that somehow it would die a natural death. However, they strongly opposed interfering with the property rights of others, a sacred right guaranteed by the Constitution. In addition, even the most liberal Northerners drew back at the idea of accepting blacks as their equals. At heart, the Northerners, like the Southerners, were racists, fearful and disdainful of the black people. They did not know what the consequences of freedom for the black people would be and were in no hurry to find out.

In spite of all the opposition, the abolitionists continued to follow the course they had set upon. They lectured, they wrote, they held meetings, and they withstood the insults and the stones. And they found that slowly, very slowly, the attacks themselves, more than anything they had said or done, began to win them sympathizers. Many Northern men and women who disapproved of the abolitionist arguments and tactics were horrified nevertheless at the violence and insults they suffered. When an Amos Dresser was publicly whipped for committing no crime, when an Elijah Lovejoy was murdered for defending freedom of the press, democracy and the civil rights of all Americans were in trouble, these whites realized. It would be a long time before large numbers of Americans would take part in the antislavery movement, but the mounting violence began to shake many out of their unconcern. The abolitionists were clearly demonstrating that as long as slavery continued, it put all other freedoms in danger.

★ CHAPTER 8 ★

The Blacks Speak Out

To make a contented slave, you must make a thoughtless one. It is necessary to darken his moral and mental vision, and, as far as possible, to annihilate his power of reason . . . It must not depend upon mere force — the slave must know no higher law than his master's will.

— Escaped slave FREDERICK DOUGLASS in his
Narrative, 1845

The black man Frederick Douglass impressed people immediately. He was tall, easily over six feet, with broad shoulders. He had long, curly hair, parted neatly on one side, and his deep-set eyes looked intense. He carried himself with dignity and assurance. And when he spoke, it was with a deep, strong voice that showed almost no trace of the dialect Northerners expected to hear from Southern blacks.

Douglass was one of many blacks whom Southern masters had dismally failed to turn into "contented slaves." Toward the end of the 1830s and during the 1840s, the ranks of abolitionist societies swelled with black men and women who had run away from slavery or managed to buy their freedom. Once in the North, they joined the white abolitionists in fighting slavery, traveling the lecture circuit, and giving firsthand accounts of slave life. White abolitionists welcomed the blacks with open arms. One abolitionist told Garrison that the public had "itching ears" to hear a black speak, "and particularly *a slave*."

The experiences the blacks described and the insights they gave their listeners stirred white audiences more than anything white abolitionists had to say. Frederick Douglass was a case in point. As he began to tell the story of his past, his audience would lean forward to catch every word, spellbound by the tragedy and vigor of the man's life.

Douglass had been born into slavery in eastern Maryland. He never knew his father, probably a white man, and saw little of his slave mother who worked some distance from him. A loving grandmother cared for the boy during his early years. When he was about seven, he began to work for his master, an overseer on a large plantation. Here the young slave learned what it was like to be so hungry he had to fight the family dog for bits of leftover food. He found out what it was like to be so cold he had to crawl into a feedbag and sleep in a closet to get some warmth. Things got better when he was sent to Baltimore to a new master. He minded the master's son and worked in a shipyard. His mistress, a religious, warm-hearted person, treated the boy like her own son and even taught him to read and write. But times changed, all too quickly. The master began to drink heavily and his wife lost interest — even turned against — her slave charge.

Douglass was sent to a town outside of Baltimore, to the master's brother. Dissatisfied with his slave's strong will, this man turned the youth over to a "Negro breaker," noted for breaking the will and arrogance of slaves. Every week, for six months, the "breaker" flogged Douglass, no matter how well he behaved. Then, one day, in desperation, the black slave turned on the white "Negro breaker" and beat him soundly until the man bled. The frightened master withdrew. "During the whole six months that I lived with Covey after this transaction," wrote Douglass later, "he never again laid the weight of his finger on me ..."

By now a longing for freedom had taken complete possession of Douglass. During the next four years, he planned and plotted dozens of possible escapes. The one that he finally chose failed, and he and five other conspirators were quickly caught and dragged behind horses off to jail. Douglass was lucky, however. His master took pity on him. Instead of selling Douglass into the Deep South, as was customary with attempted runaways, he sent the captive back to Baltimore, to his old master.

For two more years, Douglass worked as a slave, once again in the shipyards of Baltimore. This time he learned the trade of a caulker, who tightens ships against leaks. And all the while he thought about escaping, making his way to freedom in the North. Finally, on a September day in 1838, Douglass walked away from slavery. In his pocket he carried a seaman's "protection," a paper that described its owner's appearance and authorized him as a freeman. Douglass had borrowed the document from a free black sailor, who risked his own freedom by lending it. The runaway jumped a train going from Baltimore to Philadelphia, hopping on while the train was moving so that nobody would see him clearly as he boarded. A negligent train conductor did not notice that his appearance differed from the description on his protection. At Philadelphia,

Douglass took another train, and stepped off it a free man in New York.

The fugitive made his way to New Bedford, Massachusetts, where he did odd jobs to support himself. Then, while attending an antislavery rally in 1841, he was suddenly called on by abolitionist leaders of the rally and asked to say a few words about himself. Somewhat startled by becoming the center of attraction, he spoke slowly, searching for words. The words he found as he began to tell his story moved his audience to tears. After the meeting, leaders of the Massachusetts Anti-Slavery Society invited him to become a paid lecturer to travel through the North talking about what he had seen and done.

In later years, when people asked Douglass where he had received his education, he answered, "from Massachusetts Abolition University: Mr. Garrison, president." As lecturer and main attraction of the New England abolitionists, Douglass learned a great deal about style and presentation. He was especially impressed with Wendell Phillips, and watched carefully how that outstanding speaker captured his audiences. Within a short time, Douglass too could hold an audience in the palm of his hand, making it cry at his descriptions of the effects of slavery on the slave and laugh at his mockeries of slave masters and mistresses.

The former slave's popularity soon got him into trouble. People everywhere accused him of being a phony. This well-spoken, seemingly learned man could not possibly have been a slave, they said. And the fact that, in order to protect himself from his former masters, Douglass never gave details of names and places made his story even more questionable. "Better have a little of the plantation speech . . ." one of his abolitionist friends advised him. Instead, Douglass decided to publish his life, complete with facts and names, in spite of the risk it involved. His *Narrative of the Life of Frederick Douglass* appeared in 1845 and quickly became a best seller in the United States and Europe. Unlike other famous authors, Douglass met success by running away. He escaped to England to avoid possible slave catchers who would have little difficulty finding him now. There, sympathetic Englishmen and Americans raised enough money to buy Douglass his freedom. Two years after leaving the United States, he returned, a freeman under the law. Later he wrote two expanded versions of his life story, *My Bondage and My Freedom,* published in 1855, and the *Life and Times of Frederick Douglass,* published in 1881 and revised in 1892.

The black abolitionist lecturer William Wells Brown was almost as popular a lecturer as Frederick Douglass. Brown had escaped from Kentucky in 1834 and made his way into Ohio. Known only as William during all the years of his enslavement, he took the name Wells Brown from a Quaker who had helped him in his flight. Rumor had it that he was the grandson of Daniel Boone, but nobody had ever proved that. He did know that his father had been a white slaveholder; his mother, the man's slave. Light-skinned William was often taken for a white man. After his escape, Brown served as an agent of the New York and Massachusetts antislavery societies and also tried his hand at many forms of literature. In addition, he put together a fine collection of antislavery songs called *The Anti-Slavery Harp.*

Henry Bibb, another black abolitionist, made his listeners admire him for his courage as well as his intelligence. After escaping from slavery in Kentucky in 1837, he returned to the slave states to free his wife. He was captured and sold to an Indian slaveholder, but again managed to escape, this time permanently. In the North, he traveled the lecture circuit through the West, New England, and New York, often leaving his audiences weeping. The most touching part of his lectures came at the end, when he stood before his audience and softly sang "The Mother's Lament," a song the slaves supposedly sang when they were about to be sold. Bibb never managed to free his wife. During the 1850s, when fugitive slave laws were tightened, he left America and settled in Canada.

Sojourner Truth had a special place in the hearts of Northern audiences. She spoke the way they thought a slave ought to speak — in a broken dialect that had a kind of power and rhythm of its own. And her stories of sufferings were filled with a deep mystical religion that gave her the air of a prophetess carrying out the Lord's word.

Sojourner thought of herself as a missionary of God. This was why she took the name Sojourner Truth and how she got through her hardships with strength, and a firm belief in herself. Unlike the fugitives who joined her on the lecture platform, she had been a slave in the North, in Ulster County, New York, in the years before that state abolished slavery. She remembered those years well. She could describe in detail how she had been separated from her parents and her brother and sold on the auction block. She could still feel the pain she suffered after being told that the man she loved could not marry her because his master had chosen a different wife for him. And she could tell, with satisfaction, of her legal fight to free her son who had been unlawfully sold out of New York to a Southern slaveholder. Through sheer stubbornness and faith, she had won that battle. Named Isabelle at birth, she had begun to call herself Sojourner Truth in 1843. Sojourner stood for her years of wandering from place to place, first as a slave and then as a free woman. Truth was chosen, she said, because God is Truth. Under that name she lectured to audiences about slavery and worked untiringly to gain freedom and dignity for black people everywhere.

Sojourner published her life story in the 1850s as the *Narrative of Sojourner Truth, a Northern Slave*. A white friend, Oliver Gilbert, wrote the book for her, based on the old

Sojourner Truth

woman's memories and ideas. Her narrative was one of almost a hundred slave narratives that appeared before the Civil War. Like Sojourner and Frederick Douglass, Henry Bibbs and William Wells Brown published their life stories. So did many other former slaves. The Northern public devoured these books with a mixture of fascination and horror. Publishers, assured of a good profit, gladly published the works, which were often quoted and discussed in Northern newspapers and journals. Slave narratives remained popular until shortly after the Civil War. Then most of them were forgotten until almost a hundred years later when a new generation became interested in the lives and thoughts of black men and women.

Douglass, Brown, Bibbs, and a handful of other former slaves wrote their narratives themselves. Most of the others, like Sojourner, received help from white abolitionists. Only too happy to provide assistance for books that had great propaganda value, the abolitionists assigned their best writers, among them John Greenleaf Whittier, to the task. These writers used good English and proper grammar to tell the former slaves' stories for them, but they tried to keep the facts as the authors told them. And while they wrote with an emotion designed to tug at their readers' heartstrings, they tried as best they could to check out information and make sure that what they wrote really had happened. In one case, a narrative told to Whittier turned out to be so filled with exaggerations and errors that the American Anti-Slavery Society took it off the market.

Through their slave narratives, their lectures, and the examples of their lives, freemen and former slaves worked with white abolitionists to try to achieve freedom for all their people. High among their reasons for taking part publicly in the antislavery battle was their belief that if Americans saw former slaves as responsible men and women, they might become more accepting of all blacks. But the fight of these black abolitionists against deeply rooted prejudices was a long and discouraging one. Most disheartening of all was the racial bias they found among the people who claimed to care about them the most, the white abolitionists.

Few abolitionists were like Theodore Weld, who wrote, "If I ate in the City, it was at their tables. If I slept in the City, it was in their homes. If I attended parties, it was *theirs — weddings — theirs, funerals — theirs, religious meetings — theirs, Sabbath Schools — Bible Classes — theirs . . .*" Most preferred to keep social contacts down, rarely visiting blacks or joining them for social get-togethers. Sarah Douglass (no relation to Frederick Douglass), a black schoolteacher, told a sad story of attending a Quaker meeting in New York City where not one white person spoke to her, although all opposed slavery and considered themselves friends of the black people. Finally a young woman turned to her and asked, "Doest thee go out a house-cleaning?" When Mrs. Douglass explained that she taught school, the woman turned away and had nothing more to do with her.

White abolitionists often took a patronizing attitude toward black leaders, like fathers watching over children. When Frederick Douglass began adding his own philosophy and ideas to his lectures, white abolitionists acted annoyed. "Give us the facts," one of them told him, "and we will take care of the philosophy." Later, when Douglass decided to start his own antislavery newspaper, the *North Star,* in Rochester, New York, Garrison and his followers strongly advised against it.

The fact that Douglass did not take their advice led to a split between him and Garrison that ended with their not speaking to each other.

Equally irritating as this attitude to blacks was the lavish praise white abolitionists had for any black accomplishments. It was as though the abolitionists, too, believed blacks to be inferior and were surprised and delighted that they could achieve anything.

Black leaders were especially disturbed by the white abolitionists' disregard of the free blacks' needs. Although every antislavery society included aid to free blacks as one of its goals, few had the money or real interest to carry out this goal. Blacks complained bitterly that abolitionists, like other whites, would not hire black workers to any position higher than a porter or a shipping clerk, no matter how well qualified the man might be.

The free black community had always taken an active part in white abolitionist activities. Of the seventy-two persons who signed the constitution of the New England Anti-Slavery Society, eighteen were black. Six blacks served on the Board of Managers of the American Anti-Slavery Society, and blacks worked hard to organize state and local antislavery societies. As time went on, however, black leaders realized that while they must continue to cooperate with white abolitionists, they must also rely more on themselves. Throughout the 1830s and continuing into the 1840s and 1850s, blacks published their own newspapers and journals — seventeen before the Civil War. Long before whites organized vigilance committees to help runaway slaves, blacks themselves had formed all-black committees for that purpose and were successful in aiding dozens of their brethren.

Although black abolitionists participated in white antislavery conventions, they also organized separate all-black conventions. The first black convention was held in 1830, a year before Garrison began the *Liberator*. The national conventions continued every year for the next five years, and then they met at irregular intervals. Some white abolitionists criticized the separatist activities of the blacks, and some black leaders refused to attend the all-black conventions, claiming that the conventions were continuing the same type of segregation blacks were trying so hard to destroy. Leaders of the conventions answered the criticisms by pointing out that even those whites who meant well could not fully understand the special problems of the black people. For example, what was the best thing to call themselves — Negroes? Africans? Blacks? Coloreds? Each name had been used in degrading ways so often by whites that it was hard to find a term of dignity. Whites could offer little help in such areas.

The need blacks felt to achieve freedom and equality on their own terms was at the base of a black convention that shocked white abolitionists. At the convention, which took place in 1843, Henry Highland Garnet addressed his people in the most outspoken call to violence since David Walker's *Appeal* fourteen years earlier. Garnet had been eleven years old when he and his family escaped slavery in Maryland and settled in New York. He had received a fine education, and become pastor of a black church. Now, at twenty-seven, he told his black audience:

"Brethren, the time has come when you must act for your-selves . . . Brethren, arise, arise! Now is the day and the hour. Let every slave throughout the land do this, and the days of slavery are numbered . . . *Rather die freemen than live to be slaves.* Remember that you are FOUR MILLIONS!"

Frederick Douglass spoke afterward, calling for moderation rather than violence. The convention followed Douglass' lead, but rejected Garnet's speech by only a single vote.

As the years wore on, the militant words of Henry Garnet would be echoed and reechoed as black Americans grew more and more frustrated, despairing of winning a free and equal place in American society.

★ CHAPTER 9 ★

The Underground Railroad

Respected Friend — William Still: — I write to let thee know that Harriet Tubman is again in these parts. She arrived last evening from one of her trips of mercy to God's poor, bringing two men with her as far as New Castle. I agreed to pay a man last evening, to pilot them on their way to Chester county . . . I shall be very uneasy about them, till I hear they are safe. There is now much more risk on the road, till they arrive here, than there has been for several months past . . . yet, as it is Harriet who seems to have had a special angel to guard her on her journey of mercy, I have hope.

Thy Friend
THOMAS GARRETT
— from a letter by a "conductor" on the "Underground Railroad" to a Philadelphia "station," 1860

The woman was short — not even five feet — and black, and she wore a bandanna tied around her head. She walked through the slave quarters singing softly. "Dark and thorny is the desert, through de pilgrim makes his ways . . ." Her song was like a wail, her husky voice not beautiful, but haunting and urgent. ". . . Yet beyon' dis vale of sorrow, lies the fiel's of endless days . . ." She could have been any woman in her bandanna singing the slaves' songs. She wasn't. She was the woman they called "Moses." She sang her songs and slaves disappeared. They slipped away — nobody knew how — and followed her. Through dark roads and swampy lands, through thickets whose burrs clung to their clothing, they followed her. Moses led, and the people followed, all the way to the promised land of freedom in the North.

Harriet Tubman was her real name. She had been a slave and she had escaped from Maryland to Philadelphia in 1849. Gaining her own freedom had not been enough for her. She had to help her family, her friends, and finally people she had never seen before to get away too. Time and again, perhaps as many as nineteen times, she returned to the South to free her people.

She was a tender woman. She comforted the men and women who followed her without knowing where they were going. She told jokes and sang with them, trying to make them forget how frightened they were. She was a tough woman, too. When a slave cried out to turn back, she did not hesitate to point a gun at him. "You go on or die," she commanded. She was sure that any runaway who returned to slavery would put all the others in danger.

Harriet Tubman knew the routes to the North well. She had a mental map of all the steps along the way, the farmhouses and cottages where her charges could get food and fresh clothing.

"Who is it?" a farmer would ask when he heard her knock at his door.

"A friend with friends," would come the answer.

It was a code. It was her "commuter ticket" on the Underground Railroad. With her codes and her courage, she carried

Harriet Tubman (left) with a group of escaped slaves

more than three hundred slaves to freedom in this railroad
that had no tracks and no trains but somehow managed to get
its passengers where they wanted to go.

When Harriet Tubman was still a slave, she heard other
slaves talk about the miraculous Underground Railroad that
whisked people away from the South. Like the others, she
pictured a great steam engine puffing its way underground,
with strange railway stations dug into the earth.

Nobody knows how the Underground Railroad got its name.
It might have been from an incident that happened in 1831.
In that year, a slave named Tice Davids ran away from his
Kentucky master. With his master close on his heels, Davids

jumped into the Ohio River and began to swim across. The
master got a small boat and followed, keeping his eye on the
swimming slave. About five minutes after the fugitive reached
shore, the master landed. He could find no trace of Davids,
and nobody in the nearby town had seen or heard of the slave.
The puzzled master told friends that his slave must "have
gone off on an 'underground railroad.'"

After that, during the 1830s, the term came into general use,
and the Railroad took on all the trappings of a real railroad.
There were "conductors," who led slaves out of captivity or
guided them at various points in their journey. There were
"stations," where sympathetic men and women gave runaways
food and fresh clothing. There were even timetables of the
"runs," which indicated when fugitives would arrive or depart
from a particular station.

During the years before the Civil War, many activities of the
Underground Railroad were kept secret because federal laws
made it a crime for anyone to help an escaping slave. After the
war, so many legends and romantic stories grew up about the
Underground Railroad that even today students of the period
have difficulty separating myths from reality. One part of
Underground Railroad history that had long been ignored has
been rediscovered in recent years — the crucial role of blacks,
slave and free, in it.

In the prewar years, Southerners accused Northern abolitionists of conducting a highly organized national network of Underground Railroads that spirited slaves away at astounding
rates. Actually, the organization of the Underground Railroad
was haphazard, and done on a local not a national basis. In
some areas, such as Ohio and parts of Pennsylvania, abolitionists

and friends of the black people did have well-organized systems for helping fugitives. In other areas, runaway slaves had to fend for themselves or rely solely on fellow blacks for aid. Some escaping slaves knew nothing about the Underground Railroad, making their way simply on their own courage and determination.

For a slave who ran away, and for those who helped him, every step was filled with danger. First, the slave had to break out of the master's plantation or farm. Most tried to make their getaways at night, when the white folks slept. Harriet Tubman usually arranged to lead her fugitives out of slavery on a Saturday night. Because Sunday was a holiday, she had an extra day's start on her pursuers.

Runaways who had a guide like Harriet were lucky. Most did not. For them, that first step from the familiar plantation into the vast unknown was perhaps the most frightening of all. Instead of a compass to show them the way, they used their own instincts and the North Star. Fugitives had an almost mystical belief in the power of the North Star to lead them to safety. They followed it faithfully and, when clouds covered it, they desperately felt the trunks of trees for the moss that grew on the northern sides. From working outdoors, most fugitives understood the landmarks of nature, and these, too, guided them in their flight. In Kentucky and western Virginia, for example, they followed the lakes and streams that led to the Ohio River. In eastern and central Virginia, they could head toward the Appalachian Mountains northward.

Fugitives usually started out with a small amount of food and clothing, which they took from their masters and justified as part payment for the years of free labor they had given.

The first part of the journey, in the South, was usually the hardest because the runaways had almost nobody to turn to. As much as they could, they traveled at night and slept and hid during the day. Mile after mile, as they walked and ran and hid, they searched for places to rest and refresh themselves. Some took cover on other plantations, where slaves sheltered them, fed them, and sent them on their way. Some found refuge in the cabins of free blacks, who aided them at great risk to themselves. Some wandered into Southern cities, where they mingled with the free black population and often found work to earn enough money to keep going.

As a fugitive moved northward, he might make contact with an agent of the Underground Railroad who would give him the name of a friendly conductor to help him. In well-organized regions, Underground Railroad stations might be ten or twenty miles apart. At each station, the fugitive would be hidden — in a barn, an attic, a church tower — given food and provisions and then sent on his way with directions for reaching the next station. When a fugitive or group of fugitives arrived at one station, its conductor tried to spread the word to others to be prepared. Underground conductors called their secret messages the "grapevine telegraph." The hoot of an owl, a shrill bird call, or a whistle had special meaning for those people who waited, listening, for these signals of runaways. When a fugitive reached a new station, he signaled to its conductor by the way he knocked or the words he said that he was the expected visitor. Three knocks on a window might be the signal in one area. "A friend with friends" was an accepted response in another. The code words "William Penn" helped fugitives in still other areas.

Many of the fugitives went through their entire journey, from Deep South to far North, and often on to Canada, by foot. Others found ways of traveling that were easier and safer. Those who had help might be hidden and carried for part of their journey in a covered wagon or a farm wagon with special closed compartments. Or they might be stowed away on small trading vessels that moved from Southern to Northern ports. Free blacks in border states often ferried their escaping brethren across streams that led from the slave states to the free states. After real railroads came into general use, fugitives such as Frederick Douglass hopped them and presented false papers or kept out of sight. One runaway, Henry Box Brown, reached freedom via the Railway Express. He was hidden in a box and shipped as freight by the Adams Express Company from Richmond, Virginia, to Philadelphia. The trip took twenty-six hours. When Brown arrived at his destination, the Philadelphia antislavery office, he stepped through the opened lid, stretched forth his hand, and gaily said, "How do you do, gentlemen?"

Fugitives used many kinds of disguises during their escapes. Light-skinned blacks had an easier time than their darker brothers because they could pass as whites. Some men pretended to be their own masters. Occasionally women acting like mothers or nurses carried white babies lent by sympathetic whites. Other escaping slaves wore wigs, beards, mustaches, and all sorts of costumes to change their appearance. A favorite disguise was a Quaker woman's costume with its big veiled bonnet that hid its wearer's face.

Like so much else about the Underground Railroad, the routes used by escaping slaves are hard to pinpoint today. Fugi-

The Underground Railroad, a painting by C. T. Webber

tives crossed mountains, forded rivers, and pushed their way through valleys and swamps as they moved ever northward. Their routes turned and twisted, crossed and zigzagged to keep slave catchers guessing their whereabouts. Sometimes escapers would retrace the routes they had already taken, to throw a master or slave hunter off the track. A favorite trick of Harriet Tubman was to board a real railroad car going south with a band of fugitives, and then, when the time was right, move northward again. She knew that nobody would suspect fugitives of fleeing southward.

The men and women, blacks and whites, who helped fugitive slaves risked everything for people they did not know and likely would never see again. For the most part, the conductors on the Underground Railroad were simple people who did not appear on the lecture platform or take an active part in the organized antislavery struggle. Some of them were not even abolitionists or especially friendly toward blacks, but they felt sympathy and admiration for those slaves whose desperate courage led them to break away. Among the abolitionist leaders, many opened their homes to fugitives. Frederick Douglass, for example, ran an active Underground Railroad station in Rochester, New York, where he lived. He hid and protected fugitives who came to him and helped them on their way to Toronto and St. Catharines in Canada. Still, abolitionists differed among themselves about how much of their efforts and resources should be devoted to fugitive aid. The Garrisonians in particular argued that their main job was to arouse the nation to abolish slavery as a whole, and that helping individual slaves was a secondary and less important goal.

The names of most Underground Railroad workers have been forgotten, and many were never known. But a few became recognized in their own time and remained famous afterward for their humanitarian work.

At the head of any list of Underground Railroad leaders stands Quaker Levi Coffin, who became known as the "president" of the Underground Railroad. "The title was given to me by slave-hunters," he once explained. "I accepted the office thus conferred upon me . . ." Originally from North Carolina, Coffin moved to Newport, Indiana, where he put together one of the most elaborate and best-organized slave-escape systems. His own house stood on the crossroads of three routes, and fugitives flocked to him for refuge. Later, Coffin moved to Cincinnati, where he built a similar organization. In his thirty-five years as a conductor on the Underground Railroad, he helped about 3000 slaves escape.

Thomas Garrett, another Quaker, built a slave-escape organization in Wilmington, Delaware, comparable to Coffin's activities in Indiana and Ohio. At one point in his long career of helping fugitives, he was arrested and fined the steep sum of $8000, most of the money he had. "Judge," the Quaker is supposed to have said, "thou has not left me a dollar, but I wish to say to thee, and to all in this court-room, that if any one knows of a fugitive who wants a shelter and a friend, send him to Thomas Garrett and he will befriend him."

Jonathan Walker, captain of a New England merchant ship, was caught carrying a group of seven runaway slaves from Florida to the Bahama Islands. The Florida court that tried him decided to make an example of the Yankee captain. He was forced to stand in a pillory and to have his hand branded with the letters "S.S." for "slave stealer." He was also fined heavily and sent to prison, but friends paid the fine and had him released. Abolitionists gave him a hero's welcome when he returned home, with poet Whittier writing a special poem, "The Branded Hand," in his honor.

Perhaps the most adventurous of the conductors of the Underground Railroad was John Fairfield. Born in Virginia, he turned against slavery early in life. As an adult, he moved North and devoted himself to helping slaves escape. Time and again he went deep into the South, commissioned by Northern blacks to find particular slaves and spirit them away to freedom. Less idealistic than most abolitionists, Fairfield often charged for his services, although he also helped blacks who could not pay him. A master at disguises, he managed to fool whomever he met with his various poses. In one escapade, he led twenty-eight slaves to freedom as part of a made-up funeral procession.

Fairfield was one of very few whites who went from the North into the South to free slaves. Most white Underground

Railroad workers limited their activities to helping those fugitives who reached the North. Even the most outspoken foes of slavery usually considered stealing slaves from the South more of a violation of the law than they wished to take part in. They left the first stages of escape to the fugitive himself or to other blacks and believed that their responsibility came once a runaway had crossed into a free state.

Harriet Tubman became the most famous and most loved of the blacks who went into the South to shepherd slaves along escape routes. Another dedicated black guide was Josiah Henson, said to have been the model for Harriet Beecher Stowe's Uncle Tom. Born a slave, Henson had escaped to Canada with his wife and children. There he learned to read and write and helped found a settlement for fugitive slaves. From his comfortable Canadian base, Henson traveled back and forth to the South to rescue others. On one trip, he journeyed four hundred miles to avoid slave catchers in a roundabout route from Canada through New York, Pennsylvania, and Ohio to Kentucky. He gathered about thirty slaves and safely returned with them to Toledo, Canada.

Nobody can say exactly how many slaves escaped the South and settled in the North and Canada during the years of the Underground Railroad. Southerners claimed that they lost hundreds of thousands of slaves and millions of dollars of slave property because of the unscrupulous abolitionists who ran the Underground Railroad. United States census reports indicated much lower figures, perhaps about 1000 runaways a year. Students of that period estimate that about 50,000 to 60,000 slaves fled from the South to the North or Canada.

Compared to the four million blacks still enslaved, the number of fugitives who made their way to freedom was tiny. But the reaction to the Underground Railroad and its runaway slaves was much greater than the figures might indicate. Southerners grew furious at the loss of even a single slave, and abolitionists waxed triumphant at the rescue of even one fugitive. And the realities and legends of the Underground Railroad added to the divisions already threatening to separate the North and the South.

★ CHAPTER 10 ★

The "Woman Question" Splits the Abolitionists

Confusion has seized us, and all things go wrong,
  The women have leaped from "their spheres,"
And, instead of fixed stars, shoot as comets along,
  And are setting the world by the ears! . . .
They've taken a notion to speak for themselves,
  And are wielding the tongue and the pen;
They've mounted the rostrum; the termagant elves
  And — oh horrid! — are talking to men!
— by woman abolitionist MARIA WESTON CHAPMAN, 1830s

The merchants of Canterbury, Connecticut, hired Miss Prudence Crandall to open a posh private school for their daughters. They considered her a fine choice. Twenty-seven years old, nice-looking but not beautiful, Miss Crandall had the makings of a prim New England schoolmistress who was likely to remain a spinster. When she bought a large house on the village green and began running the Canterbury Female Boarding School in 1832, fathers and mothers of young Canterbury women knew they had chosen wisely.

They changed their minds within a year. Without consulting anybody in the community, Miss Crandall accepted a young lady named Sarah Harris as a student in her school. Sarah had made excellent grades in her district school, and was the daughter of a well-to-do farmer. She had only one drawback: she was black.

Prudence had thought the matter over carefully. A Quaker, she had been reared to believe slavery a sin. She had read the *Liberator* faithfully for some time and admired Garrison. While she expected some complaints about accepting a black student, she felt sure that Sarah would soon take her place among the students, and everybody would forget her color.

She was wrong. The white citizens of Canterbury went into an uproar. Without a moment's hesitation, they removed their daughters from the school, leaving the schoolmistress with a big building and one student.

Now Prudence took a step that she knew spelled trouble. She decided to turn her school into an institution for black girls only. She sought Garrison's advice in her decision. "I do not dare tell any one of my neighbors about the contemplated change in my school," she wrote him in January 1833, and then came to see him. Impressed with her courage, Garrison ran an ad for students in the *Liberator*. Samuel May offered to help her, and ever-generous Arthur Tappan volunteered funds for the school.

When word of the school spread, the townspeople grew vicious. They set up a boycott against Prudence and the twenty girls she had enrolled from various parts of New England. Merchants refused to sell them food and clothing, and doctors refused to treat them even when ill. Whenever one of them walked through the streets, town loafers followed her, shouting and blowing horns in her ears.

Finally, the townspeople found a legal way to close the school. Andrew Judson, their lawyer, pushed a ruling through the state legislature making it illegal for anyone to open a school for out-of-state students without permission from the local authorities. Since most of Miss Crandall's students came from other states, she stood in violation of the law. When she still refused to close her school, she was arrested and jailed.

Prudence spent only one night in jail, in a cell recently vacated by a convicted murderer. In that night she became a heroine to the abolitionists, the first woman martyr of their cause. "Savage Barbarity!" screamed the *Liberator*'s headlines while antislavery workers everywhere made Prudence Crandall and her girls the subject of emotional lectures.

The case was tried several times during the next year, without either convicting or clearing Prudence. The townspeople finally won their battle by breaking the school windows, setting parts of the building on fire, dumping manure in the well, and otherwise making life unbearable for the teacher and her students. At about the same time, Miss Crandall met and married a Baptist minister, Calvin Philleo, whose convictions about the education of blacks did not run as deep as hers. She gave up her school and in 1834 moved West with him. For the rest of her life, she neither spoke out publicly nor wrote about abolition or the education of blacks.

Prudence Crandall was perhaps the only woman famous in the abolitionist movement who gave up the antislavery struggle after losing on a single issue, and the only one, too, who smothered her own convictions and dutifully followed in the ways of her husband. Most female abolitionists were fighters all the way and most became as involved in achieving civil rights for themselves and for women everywhere as they did in winning rights for the slave.

Of all the ladies, two sisters, Sarah and Angelina Grimké of South Carolina, stood out as the most ferocious, most puzzling, and most frantically dedicated to the antislavery struggle.

The Grimké sisters came out of the South to save the North. As Southern belles, they had an impeccable background. Their father, Judge John Faucheraud Grimké, owned large plantations and many slaves. Their mother, Mary Smith, boasted of coming from one of the best families in Charleston. Sarah and Angelina grew up surrounded by black servants who catered to their every wish. Yet, they said later, they never could accept slavery as a natural part of life, and revolted even at a young age.

". . . I took an almost malicious satisfaction in teaching my little waiting-maid at night, when she was supposed to be occupied in combing and brushing my long locks," Sarah wrote later in regard to laws that forbade whites to teach their slaves to read and write. "The light was put out, the keyhole screened, and flat on our stomachs, before the fire, with the spelling-book under our eyes, we defied the laws of South Carolina."

The elder by thirteen years, Sarah watched over her young sister as a mother might. Neither girl was pretty, Sarah, the less attractive of the two, with her thick jaw and long, straight nose. Both kept finding themselves out of place in the gay, delicate world of Southern balls and long, lazy days. Sarah broke away first. After nursing her father during a fatal illness, she left her hometown and moved to Philadelphia, where she joined a Society of Friends. The move scandalized Charleston. It was bad enough for a single girl to live alone, but Sarah's conversion from the Episcopal to the Quaker faith convinced everybody that Miss Grimké was a strange bird, indeed.

Angelina soon followed her sister into the simple Quaker religion. Unfortunately, the society she joined in Charleston was made up of only two old men who did not speak to each other. The meetings were ordeals of silence. Nevertheless, Angelina would not give up and attended regularly each week. Finally, in 1829, she joined Sarah in Philadelphia and became a member of her Society of Friends.

For a while, Sarah and Angelina devoted themselves to prayer, good works, and a search for purity in their lives. By 1835, however, the restless Angelina had joined the Philadelphia Female Anti-Slavery Society. Sarah held back, watching her more aggressive sister with a mixture of admiration and fear for her soul. Although Quakers had long been antislavery leaders, most of them disapproved of the new abolitionists, and many began to turn away from the movement altogether now that more radical people had taken over. Sarah knew that her sister was courting the disapproval of religious Quakers by joining the abolitionist cause.

Angelina plunged ahead. In August 1835, she wrote a tortured, soul-searching letter to Garrison, whom she had never met. "The ground upon which you stand is holy ground," she wrote, "never — never surrender it." Before posting her letter, she prayed to God "to be preserved from sending it if it was wrong to do so." Finally, with trembling hands, she sent it off. Almost immediately upon receiving it, Garrison published the letter, without asking Angelina's permission. Now the wrath of Charleston society and the fury of Philadelphia Quakers descended upon her head. Garrison's introduction to the letter was labeled "the ravings of a fanatic," and Miss Angelina was condemned as a soul lost to Hell. Without deliberately planning it, she had become an abolitionist leader and the first Southern woman actively committed to the cause.

Within a short time, Angelina gained a reputation among antislavery people for her sincerity and emotional commitment to abolition. People sought her out to hear firsthand reports of the horrors of slavery, and anecdotes about her appeared in antislavery journals. Carried away by her feelings and her growing influence, Angelina wrote a pamphlet addressed to Southern women, *Appeal to the Christian Women of the Southern States.* She called on the women, whose backgrounds she shared, to set their slaves free and bombard their husbands and their state legislatures with appeals for emancipation.

"I know you do not make the laws," she wrote to her Southern sisters, "but I also know that you are wives and mothers, the sisters and daughters of those who do; and if you really suppose that you can do nothing to overthrow slavery, you are greatly mistaken."

As she might have expected, "wives and mothers, sisters and daughters" joined with husbands and fathers, brothers and sons to attack Angelina. In her hometown of Charleston, the postmaster publicly burned the pamphlet and the police warned her mother that Angelina would be jailed if she ever visited the city. The reaction was different among abolitionists. They hailed the pamphlet as a unique work, the only antislavery appeal written by a Southern woman to other Southern women. As a result of it and of her growing reputation,

Elizur Wright invited her to New York to become an agent of the American Anti-Slavery Society, to speak to women's sewing circles and other women's groups about slavery. After much thought, Angelina accepted the invitation. Sarah, who had been wavering all along in her own feelings about joining the antislavery cause, now decided to team up with her sister and devote herself to the freedom crusade.

The women descended on the Northeast in 1836 like two furies. In talk after talk, they wrung the hearts of their female audiences with tales of misery and suffering. "I stand before you as a Southerner," Angelina told one audience, "exiled from the land of my birth by the sound of the lash and the piteous cry of the slave. I stand before you as a repentant slaveholder. I stand before you as a moral being and as a moral being I feel that I owe it to the suffering slave and to the deluded master, to my country and to the world to do all that I can to overturn a system of complicated crimes . . ."

As a speaker, Angelina was the more eloquent of the two; Sarah was more awkward and self-conscious. But both managed to capture their listeners and to squeeze the last drop of emotion out of every experience, real or imagined, that they'd had with slavery. At first the sisters were invited to speak at a series of "parlor talks" run by the Female Anti-Slavery Society of New York. Soon there were no parlors large enough to hold their growing audiences, and the sisters began to give scheduled lectures in churches and meetinghouses. Only women were invited to these lectures, but Sarah and Angelina noticed that each time they spoke, more and more men seemed somehow to sneak in. Not long after they began their work as the first female abolitionist agents, they found themselves speaking to overflowing halls of "mixed audiences," with both men and women listening as though hypnotized.

And now trouble began. At a time when women did not yet even have the vote, the idea of a woman taking part in scheduled lecture tours was a daring one in itself. For the sisters to speak to mixed audiences was going beyond the bounds of proper behavior for women. Even many male abolitionists — so liberal when it came to freedom for the slave — were shocked. They had always accepted women in the abolitionist movement, but only as members of separate female antislavery societies and as aides and advisers to the men. As the Grimké sisters became more deeply involved in the abolition cause, they found themselves being drawn further and further into a battle for women's rights.

"Women ought to feel a peculiar sympathy in the colored man's wrong," Angelina told a convention of women antislaveryites, "for, like him, she has been accused of mental inferiority, and denied the privileges of a liberal education." And in answer to those who argued that a national problem such as slavery was something best left to men to handle, she said, "The denial of our duty to act in this case is a denial of our right to act; if we have no right to act, then may *we* well be termed 'the white slaves of the North,' for like our brethren in bonds, we must seal our lips in silence and despair."

They were strong words for the delicate ladies of the time, and there were more to come. When the sisters went to Boston in the summer of 1837 to lecture to abolitionists there, the matter of their activities as women and as abolitionists came to a head. Garrison had invited them, and Henry Wright, his radical companion, became their agent and guide. Wright's own enthusiasm for new causes gave added encouragement to their growing commitment to women's rights.

For each lecture that the women gave, they drew capacity crowds, often with people overflowing into hallways and foyers. Many times, they would have to use two halls or churches, with Angelina speaking at one and Sarah at the other. As their activities increased, so did the criticism directed against these "fallen women." In her diary, Angelina wrote, "We have given great offense on account of our womanhood, which seems to be as objectionable as our abolitionism. The whole land seems aroused to discussion on the province of woman, and I am glad of it."

Most aroused, it seemed, were the New England clergy. On July 28, 1837, the General Association of Congregational Ministers of Massachusetts issued a pastoral letter condemning women lecturers and the men who invited them to the platform. Without mentioning the Grimkés by name, the letter warned of "the dangers which at present seem to threaten the female character with widespread and permanent injury." Woman has "appropriate duties and influence," the letter stated. "But when she assumes the place and tone of man as a public reformer, our care and protection of her seem unnecessary . . . and her character becomes unnatural." The letter, which was circulated throughout congregations and read aloud from many pulpits, also attacked Garrison without naming him for using church pulpits to discuss "perplexed and agitating subjects." Two other letters which followed criticized Garrison more openly and linked him with the Grimkés in offending decent people.

The sisters' activities along with the clerical attack caused a rift among abolitionists that would tear their antislavery organization apart in a few years. Moderates objected to the Grimkés and especially to the introduction of women's rights into the abolitionist struggle. Garrison, Weld, and others encouraged the women's work and strongly supported equality for women.

Neither the pastoral letters nor the criticism of abolitionists stopped the sisters. Their lecture schedule became grueling. They went from town to town, leaving one meeting, taking the stage coach directly to the next place, speaking again, and going on from there to the next meeting and the next meeting. They ate little and slept, with few complaints, in drafty, sometimes dirty hotel rooms. Illness and fatigue finally brought their tour of New England to an end.

A few months later, in May 1838, Angelina Grimké married Theodore Weld, who had helped and advised the sisters throughout their lecture tours. The wedding reflected the couple's beliefs in women's rights and equality of blacks. Former slaves were invited as guests, along with the couple's many black friends. Instead of a minister, Garrison read the marriage certificate aloud. And Weld added to the marriage ceremony an attack on "the unrighteous power vested in a husband by the laws of the United States over the person and property of his wife." Angelina, Theodore, and sister Sarah moved into a house on the Hudson in New York, where they continued to write and work for the antislavery cause. After the Civil War, the sisters discovered three young black brothers who bore the name Grimké. The men turned out to be sons of their dead brother Henry Grimké and one of his slave girls. Weld and the sisters accepted them wholeheartedly as their nephews, supporting them through school and exchanging many letters and visits with them.

Like the Grimkés, other women threw themselves into the abolitionist battle and found themselves under attack as women and as reformers. Lydia Maria Child was one of them. A well-known author and wife of the editor David Lee Child, Mrs. Child had won fame for such homey books as *The Frugal Housewife*, *The Little Girl's Own Book*, and *The Mother's Book*. Then she met Garrison. "I little thought then that the whole pattern of my life-web would be changed by that introduction," she once wrote. ". . . He got hold of the strings of my conscience and pulled me into reform. It is of no use to imagine what might have been if I had never met him. Old dreams vanished, old associates departed, and all things became new." Not long afterward, in 1833, she published her first abolitionist pamphlet, *An Appeal in Favor of That Class of Americans Called Africans*. Coming from the modest and sensible Mrs. Child, the work caused a sensation. Sale of her other works dropped drastically, and in the South ladies burned her books publicly. Undaunted, Mrs. Child went on to write many abolitionist pamphlets and, during the 1840s, to edit the abolitionist newspaper the *National Anti-Slavery Standard*.

Maria Weston Chapman became known for her strong will and her organizational skills along with her feminist convictions. She kept things humming at the Boston Female Anti-Slavery Society and was forever holding women's fairs and bazaars to raise money. It was she who staunchly led the other ladies from their meeting, through the mob, and on to her house after the broadcloth mob disrupted her society's meeting in Boston.

Lucy Stone was probably the most militant feminist in the abolitionist fold. At a young age she announced to her relatives that she was going to become a professional lecturer on any cause she found worthy. The first cause she chose was anti-slavery. For that her church dropped her and she suffered the bruises and insults of angry mobs. She soon became so involved in women's rights that other abolitionists reprimanded her for neglecting the main struggle of antislavery. Eventually, she devoted all her energies to women's rights. Lucy lived by her preachings. When she finally gave in and accepted the marriage proposal of Mr. Henry Blackwell, she made him pledge that he would follow the principles of complete equality for women. She kept her maiden name after marriage, and, as Mrs. Stone, continued to lecture and work for equality for women.

As women such as Lucy Stone and Lydia Maria Child pushed their efforts for abolition and women's rights, resentment against them grew stronger within male abolitionist circles. Then, in 1840, the matter of women's place in the abolition movement reached a crisis. It happened at the annual convention of the American Anti-Slavery Society.

More than a thousand men and women had gathered for the convention in New York City. Growing differences among the delegates made the atmosphere tense as the proceedings got under way. Francis Jackson, vice president of the society, began to appoint committees to deal with the various business matters of the organization. Jackson, a Garrisonian, selected his committee members carefully, trying to be fair in naming people of opposing views to each committee. But when he appointed Abby Kelley, later the wife of extremist Stephen

Foster, as a member of the business committee, the convention fell apart. Shouts filled the air, accusations flew, and bitter feelings that had been held down for years burst out and flooded the convention. Seating a woman on an all-male committee! How much further would the feminists go?

When the dust settled, a vote was taken on Jackson's appointments. All, including Miss Kelley, were approved by a vote of 557 to 451. Almost immediately, Lewis Tappan, who had been chosen for the business committee along with Miss Kelley, refused his appointment. "To put a woman on the committee with men," he complained, "is contrary to the Constitution of the Society; it is throwing a firebrand into the antislavery ranks; it is contrary to the usages of civilized society."

Amos Phelps, once a follower of Garrison and now a firm believer in male supremacy, resigned from the society. With emotion he called on all those who had voted against Abby Kelley's appointment to resign with him. Solemnly, more than 400 delegates marched out of the meeting and down into the basement. There, they began making plans for a new antislavery society.

The years of uneasy unity had ended. What everyone called the "woman question" had split the abolitionist organization wide open.

Not all the delegates who left the convention opposed women's rights. Many felt sympathy for the women's fight on an idealistic level. What they objected to was "muddying" the antislavery battle with the "woman question." Even Theodore Weld, married to Angelina Grimké, had once pleaded with his wife not to "push your *women's* rights until *human* rights have gone ahead ..."

In addition, as the angry delegates saw the situation, at the heart of the "woman question" lay the "Garrison question," for it was Garrison, more than anyone, who had promoted the women's rights issue within the abolitionist setting. When the Grimké sisters had appeared on the scene, Garrison had taken up the women's cause with a vengeance. He supported the activities of the Grimkés and encouraged them to give public lectures. At every opportunity, he insisted on including women on various committees of the antislavery societies and other reform groups to which he belonged. And he used the pages of the *Liberator* to wage the battle for women's rights. Garrison won the support of women abolitionists with his actions, and he used them, in turn, as a power base to gain more control over the antislavery movement by influencing them to work and vote for his ideas.

Long before the annual convention of 1840, a power struggle between Garrison and his followers and non-Garrisonians had begun to shape up, with the woman issue in the middle of it. Garrison had won the first test of strength, which came in 1838 at the New England Anti-Slavery Convention in Boston. As a result of his insistence that women become members of the convention on an equal basis with men, a number of influential clergymen resigned from the meeting. But the convention, filled with Garrison's supporters, accepted his resolution on admitting women, and even elected Abby Kelley to a standing committee.

Garrisonians triumphed again at the annual meeting of the Massachusetts Anti-Slavery Society in January 1839. After learning that there was a plot at work among his opponents to capture the Board of Managers and push him out, Garrison made sure to get as many free blacks and women — his most loyal followers — as possible to attend the convention.

This time, disputes centered not only on the woman question, but also on the political responsibilities of abolitionists. Garrison had taken on strong antigovernment views. He blasted the United States government for permitting slavery to exist and condemned all government as evil and unnecessary, because governments supported wars and violence. As an extension of his attacks on government, he had come to reject all political activity, including voting, because taking part in politics, he said, was another way of supporting an "evil" government. Henry B. Stanton, a powerful administrator and leader of the American Anti-Slavery Society, led an open attack on Garrison's ideas and actions. When the verbal fighting ended, however, the Garrisonians emerged victorious again. The convention accepted an annual report Garrison had prepared which called for more rights for women and recommended an avoidance of all political activities.

The battle at the next meeting, the 1839 convention of the American Anti-Slavery Society, ended in a draw. Here Garrison won a vote to seat women delegates but lost when the convention accepted the proposal of James G. Birney that it was the duty of every abolitionist to vote, and especially to support candidates sympathetic with the antislavery cause.

By the time the 1840 convention of the American Anti-Slavery Society came around, everyone knew that the abolitionists were so deeply divided on the woman question and other major issues that nothing could bring them together again. Something else was afoot also. Over the years as local antislavery societies had gained in strength, the national society had become weaker. It received little financial support from the local groups, who used the money they raised for their own antislavery activities. By 1840, the executive committee that ran the national society had decided that the organization was useless and should be dissolved.

Garrison would have none of that decision. He determined long before the meeting to make an all-out effort to win complete control of the organization. He began by packing the convention with his women followers. He chartered a special train to carry women delegates from Massachusetts to Rhode Island, and from there he arranged for a chartered steamboat to take the delegates to New York.

As the meeting got under way and the vote on Abby Kelley's appointment to the business committee began, Garrison knew that he would easily win his goals. When Lewis Tappan and the other anti-Garrisonians left the convention hall in anger, Garrison saw to it that Lydia Child, Maria Chapman, and other women received positions on the executive committee. In high spirits he wrote to his wife, "We have made clean work of everything."

Although the women had won the day, their victory was an empty one. The national society Garrison and his followers inherited had no money, few interested workers, and a bad reputation. From now on, it would serve only as a name, with its real control in the hands of the Massachusetts Anti-Slavery Society, Garrison's stronghold.

While Garrison steamrolled his ideas across the old organization, Lewis Tappan, Amos Phelps, Henry Stanton, and almost all other members of the original executive committee retired to the basement of the Fourth Free Church, where the

Lucretia
Coffin
Mott

American Anti-Slavery Society had begun its explosive meeting. There, they planned a new organization, the American and Foreign Anti-Slavery Society. It never quite took off, remaining weaker than the old society. Not long after it was formed, most of its leaders resigned, except Lewis Tappan, who bravely tried to keep the organization going with moral and financial support from England. The society survived thirteen years, and finally died in 1853.

For the abolitionist women who fought the women's rights battle, the 1840 convention of the American Anti-Slavery Society was a triumph of sorts. Whatever satisfaction they felt in finally winning seats on the executive committee of the national society, however, was quickly shattered just a few months later. At the World Anti-Slavery Convention in London, women's rightists met crushing defeat.

A number of women had been chosen as delegates by the Pennsylvania and Massachusetts antislavery societies. Among them were Lucretia Mott and Elizabeth Cady Stanton. A highly intelligent and strong-minded Quaker, Mrs. Mott, like her husband, James, was a devoted follower of Garrison. Elizabeth Stanton, the daughter of a successful New York lawyer, had been influenced in her antislavery feelings by her husband, Henry Stanton, a disciple of Theodore Weld. Ann Phillips, wife of Wendell Phillips, had also been appointed a delegate, along with her husband.

When the delegates arrived at the London meeting, they

Elizabeth
Cady
Stanton

were told that only the credentials of male delegates would be honored. Phillips, whom Ann had warned not to "shilly-shally," put up a brave fight for the women. The ladies did their share by cornering delegates at their hotel and trying to persuade them to vote for open admission. It was useless. The women were not only excluded as delegates to the convention but were also made to sit in a separate section, screened off by a curtain.

As they left the convention, Lucretia Mott and Elizabeth Stanton decided to call a women's rights convention in the United States. It took eight years for their dream to materialize. Then, in 1848, the women organized the historic Seneca Falls Convention, the first women's rights convention in America. Both women continued to devote themselves to the dual causes of women's rights and black freedom.

Of all the women abolitionists who became caught up in the women's rights struggle, perhaps the most eloquent was Sojourner Truth. The former slave could neither read nor write, and she spoke in broken English with heavy overtones of a Dutch dialect that came from her early New York masters. But she knew how to get her message across with a simplicity and beauty that made people stop and listen. Sojourner made a point of attending and speaking at women's rights conventions. In one of her most famous talks, she answered the arguments of a group of clergymen who had invaded a women's rights convention. Her words reflected the faith antislavery women had in themselves and their knowledge that only they could help themselves. What she said was recorded by a woman who attended the meeting:

Dat man ober dar say dat womin needs to be helped into carriages and lifted ober ditches, and to hab de best place everywhar . . . Nobody eber helps me into carriages or ober mud-puddles, or gibs me any best place! An a'n't I a woman? Look at my arm. I have ploughed and planted and gathered into barns, and no man could head me! And a'n't I a woman? I could work as much and eat as much as a man — when I could get it — and bear de lash as well! And a'n't I a woman? I have borne thirteen children, and seen 'em mos' all sold off to slavery, and when I cried out with my mother's grief, none but Jesus heard me! An a'n't I a woman?

★ CHAPTER 11 ★

Abolition Enters Politics

This is a cause upon which I am entering at the last stage of life, and with the certainty that I cannot advance it far. My career must close, leaving the cause at the threshold. To open the way for others is all that I can do.

— Former President JOHN QUINCY ADAMS, 1836

The breakup of the national antislavery society in 1840 marked a turning point in abolitionist history. Until then, the antislavery crusade had been a moral and religious one, aimed at piercing the conscience of the American people. Now, politics began to dominate the movement, and antislavery agitation became a political reality. More and more, Garrison and the strict "moral suasionists" who opposed political action found themselves pushed into the background as political abolitionists took center stage.

An unexpected ally gave the abolitionists their first major political support. He was former President John Quincy Adams.

Few people had loved Adams while he served as President. He had won the election of 1824 in a strange way. He had fewer popular votes and fewer electoral votes than the man he ran against, Andrew Jackson. But because neither candidate had a clear majority, the election was decided in the House of

Representatives and given to Adams. Small and potbellied, with a bald head and teary red eyes, Adams did not attract people easily. And his cold manner, tightly clenched lips, and brutal barbs at those with whom he disagreed did not help him win friends in Congress or in the nation. By the time the election of 1828 came about, Jackson was able to win easily, leaving Adams, a one-term President, humiliated and despairing.

In his diary after leaving the Presidency, Adams wrote, "I have no plausible motive for wishing to live, when everything that I forsee and believe of futurity makes death desirable . . ." Nobody would have thought that this dejected ex-President would do anything now but retire into gloomy solitude. John Quincy Adams fooled everybody. Without ever campaigning, he won a seat as a representative to Congress in 1830. He returned to Washington, the only former President to enter the House of Representatives after completing his Presidential term. There he began a new career.

Antislavery petitions launched him on that career. Early in their struggles, abolitionists had begun to send petitions to Congress calling for an end to slavery. Quakers had taken an active part in collecting signatures on antislavery petitions and directing the petitions to Congress. For the most part, the petitions were presented in the Senate or House of Representatives and then put aside without causing much stir. As the 1830s progressed, and abolitionist activities became bolder, petitions became an increasingly important part of the antislavery strategy. In the districts and counties of towns and cities, abolitionists gathered groups of volunteers to handle petitions. They gave the volunteers packages of printed petitions, showed them how to collect signatures and then how to send the petitions to

Congress. Thousands of persons, many of them not members of any abolition societies, volunteered for the petition campaigns. Soon, waves of antislavery petitions were flooding both houses of Congress. In 1836, state and local antislavery societies sent 20,000 petitions to Congress. Two years later that number increased to 300,000.

So many petitions were bombarding the House and Senate that legislators could barely get to other work on their agenda. Among themselves they began to search for ways to put aside the petitions without having them presented on the floor. When John C. Calhoun involved himself in that search, the petition problem blew up into a major national issue and gave the abolitionists the best publicity they had ever had. Calhoun, senator from South Carolina, had long been the most influential spokesman for the Southern way of life. Throughout a political career that included being a congressman, Vice President, senator, and later secretary of state, he defended slavery as a necessary and positive way of life, and insisted on a doctrine of states' rights that would remain basic to Southern thinking for generations to come.

As petitions poured into Congress, Calhoun made them his special target of attack. "They do not come as heretofore, singly and far apart, from the quiet routine of the Society of Friends," he said in a speech before the Senate, ". . . but they are sent to us in vast numbers from soured and agitated communities." He suggested a radical method of stopping the petitions — simply rejecting them so that they never reached Congress at all. His suggestion led to heated debates in the Senate and House about slavery, the right of petition, and the power of the federal government to regulate petitions. The propaganda value of those debates that brought the antislavery battle to national attention was "worth a thousand dollars to the cause," said one abolitionist.

Calhoun's proposal was defeated in both houses of Congress, but other similar measures were adopted. The Senate decided to allow petitions to be received, but then to have them automatically rejected. The House adopted a rule that became known as the "Pinckney gag" after Henry Laurens Pinckney of South Carolina who introduced it. It ruled that any petition against slavery presented to Congress be accepted, but then "be laid upon the table and that no further action whatever be taken thereon." With the adoption of this "gag rule," John Quincy

John C. Calhoun,
portrait by
G. P. A. Healy

Adams stepped into the picture to become one of the best friends the abolitionists had.

Adams had always had "an abhorrence of slavery," but he had not been able to accept the abolitionists' demands or their methods. Now, however, he could support them in a cause in which he ardently believed, the constitutional right of petition. The American Constitution provided that "Congress shall make no law . . . abridging . . . the right of the people . . . to petition the Government for a redress of grievances." The fact that antislavery petitions could be tabled before even being presented to Congress, Adams would argue, denied that right to a large group of Americans who opposed slavery.

For Adams, the battle against the gag rule began the moment the Pinckney resolution came up for a vote. A roll call was taken on the resolution so that each congressman could give his vote. As his name was called, Adams rose from his seat shouting, "I hold the resolution to be in direct violation of the Constitution of the United States, of the rules of this House, and of the rights of my constituents." His outburst brought cries of "Order!" "Order!" from representatives around him and a reprimand from the Speaker of the House. When the roll call was completed, the resolution was passed 117 to 68. Adams girded himself for a long struggle.

From now on, in every way possible, Adams tried to force antislavery petitions into House discussions and open debate on the antislavery issue. One time he introduced a petition from some ministers who pleaded that the principles of equality stated in the Declaration of Independence be upheld in the District of Columbia. The petition was aimed at slavery in the nation's capital. But it did not fall within the Pinckney rule,

Adams insisted, because it did not speak about slavery, only about the Declaration of Independence. At other times, he summarized antislavery petitions so quickly that by the time the shouts of "Order!" "Order!" rose in the House he could answer politely, "My speech is done." On still other occasions, he refused to tell the House the contents of a petition before presenting it, as was the custom. "I refuse to answer because I consider all the proceedings of the House as unconstitutional," he would announce.

Again and again Adams insisted that he was not fighting the antislavery battle, but was defending the constitutional right of petition. To prove his point, he did not hesitate to present a petition from a group of Southerners asking that all free blacks be sold into slavery. In the same matter-of-fact way, he presented a petition from some people in Rocky Mountain, Virginia, requesting that he, John Quincy Adams, be expelled from Congress.

Adams' tactics so irritated Southern congressmen and their Northern friends that whenever he rose to speak, they quickly tried to shout him down.

"I demand, Mr. Speaker, that you put him down," one congressman would call out.

"I demand that you shut the mouth of that old harlequin!" another would join in.

"A perfect uproar like Babel would burst forth every two or three minutes as Mr. A., with his bold surgery, would smite his cleaver into the very bones . . ." wrote Theodore Weld, who attended many sessions of Congress. "Whenever any of them broke out upon him, Mr. Adams would say, 'I see where the shoe pinches, Mr. Speaker. It will pinch *more* yet.'"

At one time, in 1842, his enemies thought they had found a way to get rid of the "Massachusetts madman." Adams presented a petition from Haverhill, Massachusetts, calling on Congress to "immediately adopt measures peaceably to dissolve the Union of these States." Even before he had finished reading the petition and its reasons for wanting the Union dissolved, a commotion rose throughout the House. Some members shouted for him to be censured for introducing such a treacherous petition. Others called for his dismissal from Congress.

Suddenly, Adams found himself in a struggle for his political life. The struggle went on for two weeks, with seventy-five-year-old Adams fighting with the strength and energy of a young man. A formal resolution was entered to censure the old man. Day after day, hour after hour, Adams defended himself, the petitions he had introduced, and the Constitution of the United States. While he spoke, his words were printed and reprinted in newspapers throughout the North. For the first time, the man who had been disliked by so many began to win friends everywhere. Those who had opposed him all along now spoke with grudging admiration of "Old Man Eloquent" and "Old '76." Finally, exhausted by the thousands of words that had flowed through their chambers in recent weeks, members of Congress voted to table the censure resolution. The old man had won a great victory.

The gag rule would continue for two more years, but the tide seemed to turn after Adams' triumph in 1842. The petition campaign and the controversy it aroused began to have some effect on the public at large and on Congress itself. Northerners who had regarded the abolitionists as cranks and fanatics spoke more often now of their dedication to defending a sacred

John Quincy Adams

American right. The fact that John Quincy Adams had taken up their cause gave the abolitionists prestige they had always lacked. And the face-to-face contact they made as they knocked on doors and sought signatures for their petitions did much to help people understand what they were fighting for. Although the abolitionist societies did not greatly gain in number, the antislavery principles they had been promoting began to be talked about by millions of people.

While Adams was battling the gag rule, a group of abolitionists were forming their own political party devoted to antislavery principles. The men behind this new party had been
among those who had marched out of the national convention
of 1840. They included Joshua Leavitt, powerful leader of New
York City's antislavery society, Elizur Wright, and — much to
Garrison's dismay — John Greenleaf Whittier. Myron Holley,
editor of an abolitionist newspaper, the *Rochester Freeman*,
gave life to a loose idea these men had of forming an antislavery
third party. Holley called a meeting of abolitionists to discuss
the idea in October 1839. The proposal did not win acceptance
then, but a month later, at a larger meeting in Warsaw, New
York, a group of abolitionists decided to take the political
plunge.

The first convention of the new Liberty Party met in Albany,
New York, on April 1, 1840. Gerrit Smith, New York abolitionist and wealthy philanthropist, agreed to back the party
with large sums of money. Somewhat reluctantly, James G.
Birney, the well-known former slave owner and active abolitionist, accepted the party's nomination for President. His running mate was one Thomas Earle, a Philadelphia Quaker and
abolitionist.

The infant party had little support from anyone. Candidates
of the two major political parties, the Whigs and the Democrats, ignored the Liberty men. Garrison considered the whole
third-party movement ridiculous, if not an outright plot to
overthrow him. Other abolitionists such as Lewis Tappan and
Theodore Weld doubted whether a political party could present
abolitionist principles accurately without opening them to ridi-
cule. The result was a tiny vote of 7100 for the Liberty Party,

barely enough to be noticed. The Whigs won the election, making William Henry Harrison President and John Tyler Vice President.

Undaunted, the leaders of the Liberty Party continued to woo followers and advertise their antislavery principles. Four years after the party came into existence, in the national elections of 1844, Birney, again candidate for President, won more than 62,000 votes. In a development that shocked political observers, he took away enough votes in New York State from the famous Whig candidate Henry Clay to throw the entire election to the almost unknown Democrat James K. Polk. The abolitionists were on their way to becoming politically significant.

The growing support the abolitionists received strengthened John Quincy Adams' position in Congress. As time went on, he found that he was gaining allies within the congressional chambers and that a number of young congressmen were fighting alongside him to end the gag rule. William Slade of Vermont, Joshua Giddings of Ohio, Seth Gates of New York, and several others formed a small antislavery nucleus in Congress to keep the slavery issue before the public. These men were not abolitionists, just as Adams was not an abolitionist. They opposed slavery, however, and they opposed the attempt to silence the antislavery debate through gag rules. Over the years, they began to work closely with abolitionist leaders. Theodore Weld, John Greenleaf Whittier, and the old Quaker Benjamin Lundy spent much time in Washington conferring with the congressmen. Several of the young legislators lived at Mrs. Sprigg's boarding house near the Capitol, and here the veteran abolitionists and their new political partners planned petition strategies and discussed ways to extend the antislavery debate. After a while, the boarding house became known as "Abolition House," the planning center of the abolition lobby in Washington.

On a cold December day in 1844, Adams tasted the sweet fruits of victory. The House of Representatives voted to end the gag rule that he had fought against for so many years. When the vote became final, 108 to 60 in favor of dropping the rule, cheers broke out in the congressional chamber, and Adams' supporters rushed over to hug and congratulate the man who would not give up. "Blessed," said Adams, "forever blessed, be the name of God!"

John Quincy Adams had done his work well. Almost single-handedly he had shifted the abolitionist struggle to Washington and moved it into the heart of American politics. The march of events in the nation now would tie the antislavery issue to broader problems of national politics.

★ CHAPTER 12 ★

Civil Disobedience and a Higher Law

I cannot for an instant recognize that political organization as *my* government which is the *slave's* government
also . . . When a sixth of the population of a nation which
has undertaken to be the refuge of liberty are slaves, and a
whole country is unjustly overrun and conquered by a foreign army, and subjected to military law, I think that it is
not too soon for honest men to rebel and revolutionize . . .
This people must cease to hold slaves, and to make war on
Mexico, though it cost them their existence as a people . . .
— from *Civil Disobedience* by Henry David Thoreau, 1846

When poet Henry David Thoreau wrote his essay *Civil Disobedience,* he expressed the feelings of thousands of Americans
who felt sickened by a war that they considered unnecessary
and unjustified. It was the Mexican War, which began in 1846.
It was a war that brought the abolitionists closer than they had
ever been to the main currents of American thought.

During all the years in which the abolitionists had harped
away on the idea of abolishing slavery wherever it existed, they
had found little support for their goals among the majority of
Americans. The war with Mexico, which followed the annexa-
tion of Texas into the Union, made the extension of slavery to
new territories a central political issue. In this issue, many

Northerners found themselves agreeing with the abolitionists that slavery must be checked.

Northerners felt threatened by the growing political power of the South. They were angered that proslavery interests had not only helped bring slaveholding Texas into the Union, but had pushed the United States into the war with Mexico to maintain control of that new slave territory. They saw before them the dismal prospect of a series of new slave states spreading across their land. Everywhere in Northern towns and cities, people held meetings, prepared petitions to protest the war, and sang antiwar and antislavery songs.

In its eloquent anger, Thoreau's essay was the most powerful of the protests against the war and the slavery upon which it was based. For years to come the poet's words would influence people as they strove for freedom and peace in society without violence. Throughout the essay Thoreau maintained that any government, even a democracy, "becomes tyranny when it denies the right of the individual to be responsible for his intellectual and moral integrity." The individual, said Thoreau, has the right to refuse to obey a government or governmental action that he considers unjust. And, he explained, ". . . the only obligation which I have a right to assume, is to do at any time what I think is right." Thoreau himself was jailed briefly for refusing to pay taxes to a government that condoned slavery and war.

In his approach to government and slavery Thoreau expressed principles that had been stated by William Lloyd Garrison a few years earlier. "We cannot acknowledge allegiance to any human government," Garrison had written, "neither can we oppose any such government by a resort to physical force. We recognize but one KING and LAWGIVER, one JUDGE and RULER of mankind. We are bound by the laws of a kingdom which is not of this world, the subjects of which are forbidden to fight . . ."

By the late 1840s, Garrison had carried his own principles a step further. He insisted that by accepting slavery, the Constitution and the laws of the United States were proslavery documents. Therefore they must not be observed, and the Union of states based on them must be peacefully dissolved. The masthead of every issue of Garrison's *Liberator* blared out his new slogan, "No Union with Slaveholders!"

In a different vein from Thoreau, abolitionist poet James Russell Lowell put the thoughts and feelings of those who opposed the Mexican War and slavery into the mouth of a character he named Hosea Biglow in a series of satirical poems called *The Biglow Papers.* In the dialect of an old New England Yankee, Hosea told his readers:

> *Ez fer war, I call it murder, —*
> *There you hev it plain an' flat;*
> *I don't want to go no furder*
> *Than my Testyment fer that.*

Insisting that war was a "national crime" committed because of slavery, Hosea echoed Garrison's calls for disunion:

> *Ef I'd my way I hed ruther*
> *We should go to work an' part,*
> *They take one way, we take t'other,*
> *Guess it wouldn't break my heart.*

When the Mexican War finally ended, in February 1848, the United States came away with vast new territories in the West and Southwest. But the internal conflicts, aggravated by the war, continued and spread. By the end of the war, the two major political parties were hopelessly divided and confused over the question of slavery. The Whigs had split into Conscience Whigs, who opposed slavery and wanted to run antislavery candidates, and Cotton Whigs, who preferred to leave the slavery issue out of their political campaigns. Among the Democrats, the Barnburners, who opposed the extension of slavery into new territories, faced the conservative Hunkers, who were sympathetic to the South.

In August 1848, Conscience Whigs, Barnburners, and leaders of the Liberty Party met in Buffalo, New York, to form a new third party. By now the Liberty Party had almost fallen apart. However, Joshua Leavitt assured the Liberty men at the convention that the "Liberty Party is not dead but translated." The new party called itself the "Free Soil Party," and made its slogan "Free Soil, Free Speech, Free Labor, and Free Men." Its purpose was not to abolish slavery where it existed, but to prevent it from spreading to new territories. As candidates, the party chose former President Martin Van Buren and Charles Francis Adams, the son of John Quincy Adams.

The party made a good showing in the election of 1848, winning thirteen seats in Congress. The political abolitionists were making their mark on the nation, although they still remained a minority.

Then, in 1850, a new era opened in the fight against slavery. Indirectly, the Mexican War brought it about. After the war, nobody could agree on how to handle the country's newly acquired territories. California had organized itself as a free state and sought admission to the Union with a constitution that prohibited slavery. Southerners objected to that constitution and wanted slavery permitted in California and New Mexico. They threatened secession if the new territories were not permitted to have slavery. Northerners opposed extending slavery. They spoke of disunion unless Congress outlawed slavery in the territories.

Three elder statesmen fashioned a compromise designed to make everybody happy and save the Union. Henry Clay, known as the "great peacemaker," had been the force behind the Missouri Compromise thirty years earlier. Daniel Webster, the pride of New England, had always opposed slavery, but valued the Union above everything. And John Calhoun, now old and dying, fought with almost his last breath of life for Southern rights and the extension of slavery.

The compromise they designed became known as the Compromise of 1850. According to the compromise, California was admitted as a free state. Texas gave up much of its claim to New Mexico and, in exchange, the United States took over a number of the state's debts. Territorial governments were established for New Mexico and Utah without mention of slavery, leaving residents to decide the issue for themselves. The slave trade was abolished in the District of Columbia, but slavery was allowed to continue there.

All over the country, people cheered the compromise, and newspaper headlines proclaimed that "The Union Is Saved!" Abolitionists, however, and many Northerners with them, saw the compromise as a sellout to the South. Although they welcomed the abolition of the slave trade in the District of Columbia, they felt disheartened that the new law did not specifically limit slavery in the territories, did not abolish the domestic slave trade, and did not even restrict slavery in the nation's capital.

Most hateful to antislavery people was a part of the compromise that made it the responsibility of the federal government to track down and return runaway slaves. Known as the Fugitive Slave Law, it was designed to calm Southern fears of losing their slaves through the Underground Railroad and other escape plans and to discourage Northerners from helping fugitives. The law levied a stiff fine of $1000 on anyone caught helping a runaway, with up to another $1000 in damages and the possibility of a prison sentence. Marshals and deputies could be fined $1000 for not helping a slave owner catch a runaway. All that a slave owner needed in order to bring charges against a free black man was an affidavit swearing that the man had been a slave. Runaways who were captured were denied trial by jury. Instead of a judge, specially appointed federal commissioners would hear fugitive cases and decide on them. A commissioner was paid ten dollars if a fugitive was convicted and only five dollars if he was freed, making conviction tempting.

To abolitionists, the law seemed a denial of all justice to the black man and an open invitation to kidnapers who tried to steal free blacks and force them into slavery. They began to speak openly of something Garrison had hinted at many times, a "Great Slave Power Conspiracy" between Southern slaveholders and Northern manufacturers and businessmen. These "lords of the lash and lords of the loom," as Senator Charles Sumner named them, were working together, abolitionists said, in a secret plot to increase the power of the slave states and

Kidnaping by slave hunters

stretch the long arm of slavery into the North. Few Northerners paid attention to abolitionist talk of plots and conspiracies,
but as the 1850s progressed and new laws seemed to strengthen
the South's position, they too wondered how much farther
slavery's grasp would reach.

With the hated Fugitive Slave Law now part of the laws of
the land, abolitionists began to take stock of their position and
to plan their future actions. To guide them in the course they
believed that they must follow, they looked to their own consciences and chose to obey what they called a "higher law" than
the laws on the books of their courts.

The concept of a higher law had gained nationwide publicity
from a speech given in the Senate by William H. Seward.
Seward was not an abolitionist, but he opposed the extension
of slavery and the Fugitive Slave Law. He told his colleagues
that "there is a higher law than the Constitution which regu-

lates our authority over the domain, and devotes it to the same noble purposes."

Abolitionists interpreted the higher law to mean a law that came from God and operated within each person to guide him in doing what he believed to be right. Every individual had an obligation to obey the higher law in himself, they said, even when it conflicted with state or national laws. Backed by their belief in the higher law and in keeping with Thoreau's philosophy of civil disobedience, they now applied themselves to willfully breaking the laws of their country.

In the name of the higher law abolitionists formed vigilance committees in key cities of the North to protect fugitive slaves. Openly defying the law, the vigilance committees hid runaway slaves, warned them of the arrival of slave hunters in town, gave them food, shelter, and money, and when necessary rescued captured fugitives.

One of the most active of the vigilance committees was the Boston Vigilance Committee, run by a team of free blacks and white abolitionists. Lewis Hayden, a lawyer and fugitive slave himself, served on the executive committee. With him were such old-time abolitionists as Wendell Phillips and Dr. Henry Bowditch, and younger, newer converts to the cause. One of these was Thomas Wentworth Higginson. Still in his twenties when he joined the vigilance committee, Higginson was a strong, handsome, sometimes reckless reformer who came from one of the finest families in Boston.

A more moderate reformer, the well-known novelist Richard Henry Dana, Jr., served as attorney for the Boston committee. Dana wrote his most famous book, *Two Years Before the Mast,* after having gone to sea for two years as an ordinary seaman.

When he returned, he studied at Harvard Law School and became a lawyer with special interest in seaman's law. Once Dana had considered the abolitionists wild fanatics. Now he joined them in condemning a law that he regarded as unconstitutional.

The guiding light of the Boston Vigilance Committee was Theodore Parker, one of the country's most respected Unitarian ministers. In a group that included some of the finest minds in America, Parker stood out for his learning and perception. He knew about thirty languages, including Coptic, Icelandic, and a variety of African dialects. He had a library of more than 13,000 books, in which he studied at least fifteen hours a day. A member of the Transcendentalist Club, he had not joined the abolitionists until the 1840s. From then on, however, he became one of their most committed workers. After the passage

Theodore Parker

of the Fugitive Slave Law, he announced, "I call upon all men who love law to violate and break the Fugitive Slave Bill . . ."

With leaders like Parker, Higginson, Phillips, Dana, and others, the Boston Vigilance Committee became known throughout the North. Garrison did not take part in the committee's activities because of his unwavering belief in nonviolence, but he cheered its work from afar.

The most exciting and dangerous part of the committee's work came when a slave hunter caught up with a runaway slave. Then the Bostonians organized for action to save the fugitive.

The first successful rescue operation by the Boston Vigilance Committee came in October 1850, with the case of William and Ellen Craft. Two years earlier, this husband and wife had escaped slavery in Georgia through an ingenious scheme. Delicate, light-skinned Ellen had bandaged her face and her right arm and dressed herself in the clothes of a Southern planter. She and her "manservant" William had then journeyed first class from Savannah to Philadelphia. Whenever anybody stopped to talk to them, William explained sadly that his "massa" was quite deaf and could barely respond to anything said. In addition, his poor right arm was so crippled with arthritis that he could not sign his name at hotels or restaurants. After reaching the North, the couple had gone on to Boston, where abolitionists received them warmly and used their daring escape as an example of black intelligence and courage.

The Crafts settled into a comfortable life, with William working as a carpenter and Ellen as a seamstress. They became members of Theodore Parker's congregation, one of the few that accepted blacks. Then, one day, Henry Bowditch brought

Parker the news that two slave catchers from Georgia had come to town with a warrant to return the Crafts to their master.

The vigilance committee moved quickly. They hid William in Lewis Hayden's home and Ellen in the home of lawyer Ellis Gray Loring in Brookline. To keep the pursuers guessing, Ellen was then transferred to Parker's home.

The fearless minister wrote in his journal that he prepared his sermon that week with loaded pistols at his side. Finally, together with Loring, Parker went to the hotel where the slave catchers were staying. He warned them that "they were not safe another night" because crowds had surrounded their hotel and his committee could not guarantee their protection. The men left on the afternoon train. Shortly afterward, the vigilance committee booked passage for the Crafts to England, to keep them safe.

The committee outwitted the law once again in February 1851, and this time it was the blacks who saved the day. United States marshals seized a waiter called Shadrach at the Cornhill Coffee House and rushed him to the courthouse. Word of his arrest spread quickly to the vigilance committee and to the town's black community. Richard Henry Dana hurried to the office of the chief justice to stop the proceedings, but was put off. Soon four other lawyers of the vigilance committee arrived at the courthouse and managed to get a delay to prepare their defense. Suddenly the door of the courtroom where Shadrach was being held flew open and fifty blacks shoved their way in. Lewis Hayden had assembled them and was with them now. Before anybody could stop them, the men grabbed Shadrach, lifted him high in the air, and carried him off to the street, nearly tearing all his clothes as they passed him from one to another. Outside, his rescuers put the stunned fugitive into a carriage which drove him to Cambridge. From there he was sent to Vermont and then on to Canada.

Lewis Hayden, a black lawyer named Robert Morris, and several other black and white vigilantes were accused of plotting the rescue and brought to trial. After three weeks, the case was dismissed because the jury could not reach a verdict. One juror stubbornly insisted on acquitting the men.

Years later, Dana met a quiet man who looked vaguely familiar. The man reminded him that he had been the twelfth juror in the Shadrach case. When Dana asked why he had opposed conviction, the man answered that he was the person who had driven Shadrach over the line to freedom in Canada.

The Thomas Sims case came up just a few months after the Shadrach rescue, but this saga ended in disaster. Seventeen-year-old Sims had escaped a Georgia master and come to Boston. As he walked through the black section of town one night, two officers seized him and rushed him to the courthouse, where sixty-five men were assigned to guard him. No amount of arguing or legal maneuvers by Dana, Loring, or other vigilantes could help the youth. And no sudden mob of black men swarmed in to carry him to freedom. Dozens of blacks had fled the city after the Shadrach escapade. Three offers to buy Sims back were turned down by his master, who was determined to make an example of the slave.

Finally, admitting defeat, the vigilantes marched behind Sims and his escort of three hundred soldiers and policemen through the streets of Boston to Long Wharf. There a boat stood ready to carry him on his sad trip back to Georgia. Some of the abolitionists carried a coffin draped in black and printed with the word LIBERTY. Others shouted again and again, "Shame! Shame!" As the young man walked up the gangplank of the boat, with tears streaming from his eyes, someone called out to him, "Sims, preach liberty to the slaves." Then he sailed away.

The Boston Vigilance Committee suffered an even more crushing defeat in the case of Anthony Burns. But that defeat brought them more publicity and more sympathizers than any of their successes.

Burns was working in a clothing store in Boston when he

Placard written by Theodore Parker after the return of Thomas Sims to slavery

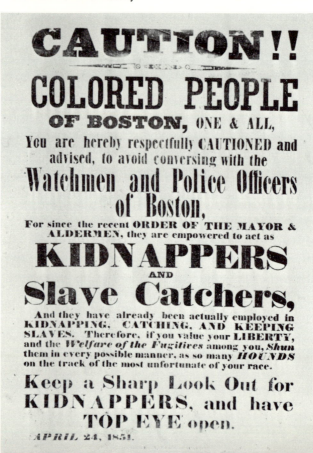

was seized in May 1854 and accused of being a runaway slave. That night his former master visited him in his cell and urged him into a confession. Realizing that they had no chance of legally saving Burns, his lawyers, Dana and Morris, joined with other vigilantes in plotting a rescue. A hasty and risky plan was worked out, with little attention to details of timing and coordination. A large protest meeting would be held at Faneuil Hall, and while it went on Higginson and a group of men would rush the courthouse where Burns was being held. The Faneuil Hall speakers would rouse the audience and send them out to help Higginson and his group, and the fugitive would be spirited away in the commotion.

The plan failed almost before it got under way. The Reverend Higginson and his group did rush the courthouse, armed with revolvers, axes, and meat cleavers. There, more than fifty men fought them back. A guard was killed, and Higginson wounded on the chin. Police reinforcements arrived shortly after the Faneuil Hall crowd did, and the rescue fizzled out.

Feelings ran high in Boston after that as blacks and whites waited nervously for the decision of Commissioner Edward G. Loring, who was trying the Burns case. When the commissioner ruled in favor of Burns' master, shopkeepers throughout the city closed their stores and draped their windows in black. Once again, on a hot June morning, crowds gathered to watch a freeman being returned to slavery. This time police lined the streets all the way from the courthouse to the wharf where a cutter waited to carry Burns to Virginia. A mounted cannon led the way, followed by an artillery battalion, a platoon of Marines, and the marshal's armed guard. In the center marched Burns, alone, head held high. And along the sides, fifty thousand men, women, and children watched the procession. "There was lots folks to see a colored man walk down the streets," said Burns.

The story had a happier ending than would have seemed possible on that bleak day. Burns was sold to a new master after he returned home. The master then agreed to sell him to a group of Boston philanthropists. Shortly afterward, Burns entered Oberlin College to study for the ministry. Less than a year after the Burns capture, Massachusetts passed a strong Personal Liberty Law that made the Fugitive Slave Law almost impossible to execute in that state. Ordinary people had been caught up in the Burns case and looked with new sympathy and understanding at the once hated abolitionists.

The final act in the drama during that summer of 1854 was played on the Fourth of July by William Lloyd Garrison. Before a solemn audience, he burned a copy of the Fugitive Slave Law and of Commissioner Loring's decision against Burns. Then he held up a copy of the United States Constitution, slowly placed it in the fire, and watched while it turned to ashes.

"So perish all compromises with tyranny!" he cried out. "And let the people say Amen."

"Amen," the voices around him repeated.

Earlier, Garrison had used the words of the prophet Isaiah in calling the Constitution "a covenant with death and an agreement with hell." Now he made his final break with that "pro-slavery document" and with the government that was based upon it. He would live only by the "higher law" within himself. And he would call with increasing urgency for disunion, a complete and final "separation between the Free and the Slave States."

For all the publicity of the fugitive rescues, for all the drama and pathos of the failures, it took a work of fiction to rouse in Northerners the depth of emotion abolitionists had been trying to kindle over the years. A housewife who had little contact with slavery wrote the work that caused a sensation throughout the country and the world. She was Harriet Beecher Stowe with her famous book, *Uncle Tom's Cabin*.

Mrs. Stowe was no rebel. The daughter of Lyman Beecher, she grew up in an educated, literary household that emphasized moderation. She did not join abolitionist societies or take part in feminist movements. Yet she managed to produce a book that spread the antislavery creed as nothing before it had. The work first appeared in serial form in the antislavery paper the *National Era,* beginning in 1851. Published in book form in March 1852, it became an immediate best seller. Within three weeks after publication, 20,000 copies were printed, and 300,000 copies came off the press during the first year. The book was translated into almost every European language. Dozens of plays based on it helped spread its message.

Millions of readers read and reread the story of the gentle slave Uncle Tom, of the cruel Simon Legree, and of the daring escape of Eliza. Mrs. Stowe had based her information on a visit to a Kentucky plantation and on data gathered from Theodore Weld's book *Slavery As It Is.* Married to an Oberlin professor, Calvin Stowe, she learned much about Underground Railroad activities from what she saw and heard from Oberlin students and faculty members. Later readers would consider her characters stiff and unreal, her moral lessons too sticky and heavy-handed. Later generations of blacks would look down on her Uncle Tom as a man who knuckled under to white people and did not exert his own individuality. They would use the term "Uncle Tom" to mean a weak black who sought to please whites. Later critics would accuse her of creating stereotypes in which blacks were easygoing and undemanding and in which those of lighter skin showed more intelligence

Harriet Beecher Stowe

than darker ones. The people of her own day saw little of that, however. They saw only the evils of slavery as Mrs. Stowe painted them, and the evils came out more clearly because she took pains to show some slaveholders as kindly and some Northerners as immoral.

The success of Mrs. Stowe's book delighted abolitionists, who recognized its great propaganda value. Only one point disturbed them, especially black abolitionists. That was the importance the novel gave to colonization. In the book George Harris speaks of his longing for Africa, even though he and his family have escaped safely to Canada. Harris and his family and several other former slaves finally do migrate to Liberia, as though Mrs. Stowe is assuring her readers that once freed, blacks themselves will choose to return to Africa. In answer to criticism, Mrs. Stowe is said to have told one black that if she could write the book over, she would not send Harris to Liberia.

Southerners regarded *Uncle Tom's Cabin* as an outright declaration of war. They wrote dozens of replies to the book and produced scores of novels to counteract its picture of Southern life. Nothing they turned out, however, could come anywhere near the popularity and impact of Mrs. Stowe's work. Along with the Mexican War, the Compromise of 1850, the Fugitive Slave Law, and other events of the 1850s, it was one more step in bringing on the Civil War and in changing the public's view of the abolitionists as traitors to a belief in them as patriots.

★ CHAPTER 13 ★

Bleeding Kansas and a Bloody Beating

Take down your map, sir, and you will find that the Territory of Kansas, more than any other region, occupies the middle spot of North America . . . Against this Territory, thus fortunate in position and population, a crime has been committed, which is without example in the records of the past . . . It is the rape of a virgin Territory, compelling it to the hateful embrace of slavery; and it may be clearly traced to a depraved longing for a new slave State, the hideous offspring of such a crime, in the hope of adding to the power of slavery in the national government . . .

But this enormity, vast beyond comparison, swells to dimensions of wickedness which the imagination toils in vain to grasp, when it is understood that for this purpose are hazarded the horrors of intestine feud not only in this distant Territory, but everywhere throughout the country. Already the muster has begun. The strife is no longer local, but national. Even now, while I speak, portents hang on all the arches of the horizon threatening to darken the broad land, which already yawns with the mutterings of civil war . . .

— Senator CHARLES SUMNER of Massachusetts in his
"Crime Against Kansas" speech, 1856

On a warm day in May 1856, a scene almost beyond belief took place in the usually dignified United States Senate chamber. Senator Charles Sumner staggered around the floor. Blood gushed from his head, soaking his shirt and jacket and forming crimson streaks across his face. Two deep gashes cut across his head to show the bone of his skull. Soon, his arms and legs would swell in purple welts where blows had beaten down upon them. Above the senator towered a tall, powerful man whose young-looking face was tight with anger and hatred. In his hand the tall man held the broken remains of a blood-soaked cane with a gold handle. U.S. representative Preston S. Brooks had used his cane deliberately to lay low his victim. He had attacked, not on the spur of the moment or in a sudden fit of rage, but only after days of planning to determine the most strategic time and place to give the event the greatest effect.

There were some who said that Sumner got no more than he deserved that day. The senator from Massachusetts had a way of turning people against him. Perhaps it was his Puritan righteousness. He came from an old New England family and carried himself with the pride of a man whose heritage and upbringing were beyond reproach. Perhaps it was his enormous ego that made Sumner unpopular. He seemed always to believe himself right and was unwilling to listen to anyone else's point of view. Tall and attractive, he did not marry until he was in his fifties, and then the marriage ended in divorce after just a few months. One Washington wag explained that his wife could not stand living with God. Or perhaps it was Sumner's unyielding idealism that annoyed people. Once devoted to a cause, he would not sway from it right or left or accept compromise in any form. "For myself," he once said, "if two evils are presented to me, I will take neither."

Sumner's pride, his ego, and his idealism had brought him to the unhappy position in which he now found himself. A long chain of events had led to this moment. And slavery had been the spark that had set those events in motion.

The senator had been a foe of slavery for years. In fact, his outspoken attacks on the institution had made him an outcast from most of Boston's high society while winning him the respect of other opponents of slavery. Sumner was one of the few whites of his time who truly believed in giving the blacks not just freedom, but equality too. Using arguments that would be echoed almost without change a hundred years later, Sumner challenged school segregation laws in Boston in 1849. He lost the case he was arguing, but six years later the Massachusetts legislature did outlaw racial segregation in state public schools.

The *Liberator* had been the first paper Sumner ever subscribed to. He had never been satisfied with it, however, because of its "vindictive, bitter & unchristian" tone, he wrote. And while he was friendly with Garrison, Phillips, and other abolitionists, he did not join the abolitionist band himself. He firmly believed that slavery must end legally, through constitutional means. Sumner maintained that the Constitution gave the states, not Congress, the right to legislate slavery matters within their areas so that Congress could not legally abolish slavery in the states in which it existed. On the other hand, because the Constitution did not specifically give Congress the power to extend slavery or protect it, he said, it was unconstitutional for Congress to establish slavery in new territories or protect slave owners through such laws as the Fugitive Slave Law.

Charles Sumner

It was on the principle of containing slavery, rather than abolishing it, that Sumner won his seat in the Senate in 1851. Twice before, he had run for office on the Free Soil ticket and been defeated. This time a coalition of Free Soilers and Democrats who opposed the Fugitive Slave Law brought him victory. In Congress, he joined a small group of men who were becoming known as the "Radicals" because of the stand they took against slavery. In the Senate there were William H. Seward of New York, John P. Hale of New Hampshire, and Salmon

Chase and Benjamin Wade of Ohio. The House had such antislavery congressmen as Joshua Giddings of Ohio, Thaddeus
Stevens of Pennsylvania, and — perhaps most dedicated —
Owen Lovejoy of Illinois, brother of the martyred Elijah Lovejoy. Later these men along with several others would become
the "Radical Republicans" in the Republican Party, pushing
for strong antislavery measures before the Civil War and for
a strict reconstruction policy afterward.

When Sumner entered the Senate, the Fugitive Slave Law
was still the main target of antislavery men, who tried in every
way possible to have it repealed. Within a few years, attention
shifted to a new problem that was really a continuation of old
ones that had been dividing the country: the problem of
whether to permit slavery in new territories, particularly the
area that was soon to become the territories of Kansas and
Nebraska.

The Missouri Compromise of 1820 had prohibited slavery in
all new land north of the parallel 36° 30', except for the state
of Missouri, and the Kansas-Nebraska region fell within that
ruling. As the nation expanded westward, however, Southern
fears had grown that the country would become over-
whelmingly antislavery, and Southern interests would be ignored. When the new territories were about to be opened for
settlement, Southerners decided to strike for a change in the
law. They found a powerful ally in Senator Stephen A. Douglas
of Illinois.

Short, feisty Douglas with broad shoulders and a hig head
had won the nickname "Little Giant" among his colleagues
in the Senate. He had also won the responsible position of
chairman of the Senate committee on territories. His keen

mind led him to see clearly to the heart of matters, and his intense ambition brought him a burning desire to be President one day. With an eye to winning Southern support and keeping his own party, the Democrats, strong, Douglas introduced a bill in January 1854 proposing that all new territories be settled on the basis of "popular sovereignty." That meant that the people in the region would decide among themselves whether, when the time came for them to apply for statehood, they wanted to enter the Union as a free state or a slave state. To make Douglas' system legal in the area that would be Kansas and Nebraska, Southerners attached an amendment to his bill repealing the Missouri Compromise.

The bill and its amendment brought a powerful reaction from abolitionists, antislavery congressmen, and the Northern man in the street. Although Douglas argued that the climate and geography of the new territories did not lend themselves to slavery and that his bill was simply a way of appeasing the South, his opponents could see only the dark shadow of the "Slave Power" blighting their virgin lands. Almost immediately, Sumner, Chase, Giddings, and several other antislavery lawmakers prepared a devastating "Appeal of the Independent Democrats in Congress to the People of the United States" in which they labeled Douglas' bill "a criminal betrayal of precious rights."

The widely circulated appeal hit its mark. Throughout the North, men and women petitioned Congress to keep slavery out of the new territories. In Boston, more than 3000 businessmen — many of them long-time opponents of the abolitionists — met in Faneuil Hall to protest Douglas' bill. Heated debates took place in the Senate. Douglas referred to the Radical sen-

ators as "abolition confederates," who represented "Abolitionism, Free Soilism, Niggerism in the Congress of the United
States." At one point Senator Wade shouted in return, "You
may call me an Abolitionist if you will . . . for if an undying
hatred for slavery and oppression constitutes an Abolitionist, I
am that Abolitionist." The country had moved a long way from
the days when "abolitionist" was a word to be whispered in the
inner parlors of a few homes or to be spat out in disgust.

In spite of all protests, the Kansas-Nebraska Act with the
repeal of the Missouri Compromise became law in May 1854,
helped on its way by the support of President Franklin Pierce.

About three months after the passage of the bill, the Republican Party was born. Three groups would exert influence
within it: radicals like Sumner and Chase, who opposed the
extension of slavery and refused to compromise again with the
South; moderates, such as the still-unknown Abraham Lincoln,
who opposed slavery but were willing to work with the South
in order to avoid a breakup of the Union; and conservatives,
who were less interested in the slavery issue than in economic
and social problems. The new party crossed all the old party
lines, including former Free Soilers, Whigs, and Democrats.

Meanwhile, in the Kansas-Nebraska area, a race was going
on. Missourians, bordered on one side by a free Iowa, were
anxious to see slavery extended to other border regions. Impa-
tiently, they had massed along their state lines, waiting to stake
their claims and the claims of slavery in the new territories
as soon as they were opened. They hoped that by sheer numbers they could take over. They were met, however, by other
settlers, as determined to keep slavery out as the Missourians
were to force it in. The settlers came from many areas, from

Kentucky, Ohio, Pennsylvania, and the New England states. Some were adventurers, some were frontiersmen looking for rich new lands, and some were stubborn and dedicated men and women willing to make any sacrifice to keep Kansas and Nebraska free states.

A former school principal named Eli Thayer conceived of a plan to send New Englanders to the Kansas-Nebraska region to save it from slavery. Thayer organized the Massachusetts Emigrant Aid Company, which later became the New England Emigrant Aid Society. It raised money to transport settlers to Kansas and to finance schools, churches, and homes for them there. Established as a stock company designed to make money for its investors, it quickly gained a reputation as a symbol of the Free Soil struggle.

Far from an abolitionist, Thayer considered Garrison "irresponsible," and maintained that the abolitionists should be "shunned as though they had been lepers." Garrison, in turn, complained bitterly that of the more than 1000 people who signed up with the society shortly after it began, almost none was an abolitionist. Still, Garrison and other abolitionists hailed the hardy settlers who went out to conquer new territory. The ever-daring Higginson personally escorted a group of settlers to the territory and traveled around it. Later he wrote, "Ever since the Rendition of Anthony Burns in Boston, I have been looking for *men*. I have found them in Kanzas . . . A single day in Kanzas makes the American Revolution more intelligible . . ."

Although neither Garrison nor Thayer regarded the New England settlers as abolitionists, Missourians who opposed them were convinced that each and every Yankee in the territory was out to abolish slavery in the new lands and in the old South. To stop them, Missourians tried to steal territorial elections. Each election day, when settlers voted for territorial delegates to Congress, wild throngs of Missourians crossed the border, voted for proslavery candidates, and then returned to their own land. Northerners called them "border ruffians" and Northern newspapers described with moving emotion the violence and atrocities they committed on the now "bleeding Kansas."

To help their settlers, New Englanders raised money and began to smuggle rifles to the pioneers. Some of the wealthiest and most aristocratic New Englanders found themselves defying a government ban on weapons and devoting themselves to collecting money and arms. Higginson, Phillips, and Gerrit Smith joined with Dr. Samuel Cabot and Boston preacher Henry Ward Beecher, son of Lyman Beecher, in fund-raising campaigns to arm the immigrants. Beecher's contribution included Bibles along with rifles, inspiring the nickname "Beecher's Bibles" for the weapons.

By 1856, people were speaking of the Kansas struggle as "civil war." Disputes that might have been taken for granted in the rough and tumble world of other frontiers here came to stand as symbols of the national agony over the slavery question. Against this background, Charles Sumner gave his "Crime Against Kansas" speech in the Senate and soon found himself in a bloody heap on the floor. The very day that Sumner began his speech, May 19, 1856, Missourians were marching on the city of Lawrence, where they would destroy a new hotel and burn dozens of homes.

Sumner had spent two weeks preparing his speech, which he presented over two days, speaking more than eight hours in all. It was a strange speech. It blasted the administration of President Pierce, the Missourians, and the supporters of slavery with a combination of angry, almost earthy words and flowery references to Greek, Roman, and British poetry. At several points in the talk, Sumner directed carefully thought-out barbs and personal attacks at three proslavery senators; Stephen A. Douglas, Andrew P. Butler of South Carolina, and James M. Mason of Virginia.

Northerners hailed the speech as a masterpiece. Southerners fumed at its criticisms, and especially the brutal personal attacks it had included. One Southerner, congressman Preston S. Brooks of South Carolina, took the attacks more personally than most. Brooks was Butler's relative, and felt himself and his family deeply insulted by the senator's speech. In keeping with Southern tradition, he vowed to restore his family's honor. A gentleman's duel might give the impression that he considered Sumner his equal. A beating — as though Sumner were a lowly slave — would let the nation and the world know that the senator was his inferior.

Brooks bided his time until he could find the right moment to strike. That came on Thursday afternoon, May 22. After waiting for the chambers to clear when the Senate adjourned, Brooks approached Sumner, who was working at his desk.

"I have read your speech twice over carefully," he told the senator. "It is a libel on South Carolina, and Mr. Butler, who is a relative of mine."

Before Sumner could respond, Brooks began beating him over the head with the gold-handled cane he had selected for the occasion. Stunned, Sumner tried to defend himself. But he was no match for Brooks, who beat on relentlessly. Bruised and bleeding, Sumner began to collapse on the floor just as two congressmen who had heard the commotion rushed in. One grabbed Brooks and held him while the other caught Sumner and saved him from a hard fall. A number of Southern senators had witnessed part of the attack, but none had made a move to help Sumner.

The senator was quickly patched up and taken home, where a doctor treated him. "I could not believe that a thing like this was possible," he mumbled as he fell into a deep, exhausted sleep.

News of the beating knocked the breath out of a nation that was witnessing new bursts of violence every day. Northern newspapers raged against the brutality of the South, and hundreds of people, young and old, wrote letters of sympathy to Sumner. Everywhere, political rallies were held and speakers condemned the techniques of the Slave Power. Southerners saw the situation differently. Almost to a man, they hailed Brooks' action. Groups of people sent him canes, one of them from South Carolina merchants inscribed "Hit him again!" Like Sumner, Brooks received hundreds of letters, most of them praising him. A special committee of the House of Representatives investigated the incident and recommended the expulsion of Brooks. Failing to get the necessary two-thirds vote for expulsion, the House censured Brooks instead. Instantly, he resigned and almost immediately was reelected by his constituents. When his case came to court, he was fined $300 and freed.

It would take Sumner more than three years to recover enough from his caning to take his seat again in the Senate on a regular basis. During that time, his empty chair would stand as a symbol of his martyrdom and a reminder to the people of the times in which they lived.

Bleeding Kansas and Bleeding Sumner became the theme of the Republican Party campaign during the national election of 1856. The young party held its first national convention in that year. Radicals like Sumner had cause to cheer that part of the party's platform that called on Congress to outlaw slavery in the territories and to admit Kansas immediately as a free state. Abolitionists like Lewis Tappan complained, however, that the chairman of the convention was Francis Blair, a slaveholder, and that the party's platform did not mention the Fugitive Slave Law, slavery in Washington, D.C., or the domestic slave trade. The convention nominated John C. Frémont for President.

In the campaign, Frémont faced James Buchanan of the Democratic Party and former President Millard Fillmore, nominated by a new party called the Know-Nothings, which had replaced the Whigs. Barely noticed during the elections was another party, whose members called themselves the Radical Abolitionists, made up of a sprinkling of old Liberty Party members. Frederick Douglass took an active part in organizing this party, the only one that called for the full-scale abolition of slavery. At the last moment, however, Douglass threw his support to the Republicans. Like other voting abolitionists, he decided to settle for less than best rather than waste his vote on a party that had no chance of winning. Even Garrison, who still opposed voting in political elections, gave some support to the Republicans. If there were no moral barriers to voting, he wrote in the *Liberator,* "and we had a million votes to bestow," he would give those votes to Frémont.

Frémont won over a million votes but they were not enough to give him the election, which went to Buchanan. Still, the good showing of his party gave hope to antislavery forces and struck fear into the hearts of Southerners.

Now a new turn of events in Kansas would raise that fear to a level unknown before. The fear would focus on a middle-aged white man who became the most controversial and problematic of all the abolitionists Southerners had fought over the years. He was John Brown of Osawatomie.

Handbill against the
new Republican party
and its abolitionist candidate,
John C. Frémont

★ CHAPTER 14 ★

Abolition Turns to Guerrilla Warfare

I John Brown am now quite *certain* that the crimes of this
guilty, land: will never be purged *away;* but with Blood.
I had *as I now think: vainly* flattered myself that without
very much bloodshed; it might be done.
— last message of JOHN BROWN before being hanged, 1859

To people of his own era and to people who came later John
Brown was a figure of mystery and controversy. Those who
came to worship him after his death compared him to Jesus
Christ. Jesus, too, had been unknown for most of his life before
he stepped forth among his people to create a revolution for
all time. And Jesus, too, had died a martyr, misunderstood by
all but a few followers. Those who condemned John Brown
would say that he was more a bitter, desperate man than a
sainted martyr. They would point to his cold-blooded cruelty
and say that he behaved like a madman. Mental illness, many
people said, ran in his family.

Many factors came together in the creation of John Brown's
character. The strict religious atmosphere in which he grew up
led him to judge everything in terms of right and wrong, with
no way in between. If slavery was wrong, then everything done
to defeat it was right. His lack of success in business life built
within him a resentment toward the outside world and en-

couraged a turning into himself. Eventually, he would see himself as a prophet destined to change the world that had paid him so little attention. The free, often lawless atmosphere of the frontier in which he lived encouraged his individualism and his inclination to solve problems in his own way, without regard for established institutions. Finally, the climate of violence and hatred that gripped his age added fuel to the fire of anger and bitterness growing within him.

In some ways, John Brown and William Lloyd Garrison represent two sides of the same coin. Both have been seen as fanatics, so driven to achieve their ends that they were willing to use almost any means. Both guided themselves by a higher law than the written laws of society; for both, what they considered right was more important than what the law said was right. Both were passionate men, with tendencies toward violence. They differed in how they handled those tendencies, and it was their differences that gave each his unique role in the antislavery drama. Garrison turned his violent impulses into thousands of bitter words that filled the pages of his newspaper and echoed through the lecture halls of the North. He kept a tight hold on any inclinations he might have had toward physical violence by devoting himself to principles of nonviolence and directing his energies to moral warfare. Brown, on the other hand, allowed violence to rule his life. He could accept and justify the violence in which he engaged because it was in the service of a cause that to his mind outweighed all other considerations in life — the destruction of slavery. The violence he embraced made him, ultimately, the more radical of the two men.

John Brown came from a humble family. His father, hard-working and pious, earned a living as a tanner, shoemaker, and farmer. His mother was the daughter of a Congregational minister. Brown was born on May 9, 1800, in Torrington, Connecticut. The boy was reared in a rigid Calvinist tradition that left little time for fun or play. Any kind of mischief was punished with solid whippings so that the child would always remember his father's lessons to "fear God and keep his commandments."

Brown's father hated slavery and taught his son that it was an evil sin. Once the youth spent some time with a landlord who owned a slave about his own age. Brown wrote later that while the landlord "made a great pet" of him, the man neglected his slave, who was "badly clothed" and "poorly fed." When the landlord beat the black boy with an iron shovel, Brown was so horrified that he swore "*Eternal war with slavery.*"

Early portrait
of John Brown

As he grew to manhood, the sinfulness of slavery became almost an obsession with Brown. The abolitionist crusade began to gather steam while he was in his early thirties, and the young man listened intently to what the crusaders had to say. He read the *Liberator*. Too independent and too orthodox in his religious views to become a follower of Garrison, he nevertheless admired that outspoken reformer. Later he adopted Garrison's antislavery arguments as his own.

In Ohio, where he lived for some years, Brown took an active part in fighting the state's restrictive Black Laws and in hiding fugitive slaves who came to his Underground Railroad station. By the time of Elijah Lovejoy's death in 1837, he was ready to vow before a hushed congregation that had gathered to protest the murder that he would now dedicate his life to the destruction of slavery.

He did not say how he would accomplish his mission, and it was not until 1847 that he gave even the slightest hint of the kind of tactics he would later follow. By then, Brown had moved his growing family to Springfield, Massachusetts, and there he invited Frederick Douglass, then on a lecture tour of New England, to visit his home. The two men impressed one another, Douglass later describing Brown as "lean, strong and sinewy, built for times of trouble."

Brown outlined for Douglass a plan for guerrilla warfare that he had been working on to end slavery quickly. Squads of armed men would hide out in the Allegheny Mountains that cut through Southern states and from there dip down into fields and plantations and stir slaves to run away. Some of the runaways would remain in the mountains to help other slaves and harass slaveholders. The scheme, said Brown, would make slaveholders so insecure that the value of their human property would go down, and slavery would die out.

Douglass had many doubts about the plan, but Brown's intensity and his insistence that slavery could be destroyed only through bloodshed shook Douglass' belief in Garrison's principles of "moral suasion" and nonviolence.

In 1851, Brown organized a group of black friends in Springfield into a secret band to protect members against the Fugitive Slave Law. He named the group the United States League of Gileadites, after Mount Gilead in the Old Testament. In a document he called "Words of Advice" he warned members of his League that they were to go about armed and be prepared to shoot if a slave catcher tried to take any one of them. The Gileadites never saw action and probably never saw any slave catchers, who were rare in Springfield.

After years of attempting and failing at various businesses — tanning, farming, sheep raising, land speculation — Brown joined five of his sons and other Free Soilers in the Kansas-Nebraska region in 1855. Before going, he appeared at a convention of Radical Abolitionists, attended by Gerrit Smith, Frederick Douglass, Lewis Tappan, and other old Liberty men. With much emotion, he read them a letter from one of his sons in Kansas pleading for weapons and ammunition with which to fight proslavery forces. With the money delegates contributed and weapons rounded up from Ohio friends, Brown set off for Kansas and the start of a new life. Behind him in North Elba, New York, now, he left his wife, daughters, and youngest son. The family would still be living there four years later when John Brown's body was brought home to rest.

For Brown, Kansas became a testing ground for ideas and an

escape hatch for the pent-up emotions within him. He became known to the region, and to Northerners, through a series of skirmishes — some harmless, some gruesome bloodbaths. During his first Kansas winter, in December 1855, Brown and his sons rushed from their settlement near the town of Osawatomie to the city of Lawrence to help put down a threatened invasion by Missourians. The crisis ended with antislavery and pro-slavery forces accepting a peace treaty before any blood was spilled. Although he saw no action, Brown was named a captain of the "First Brigade of Kansas Volunteers" by the head of the antislavery forces, Dr. Charles Robinson, who was impressed with his zeal and his fine array of weapons.

Captain Brown did not have to wait long for real fighting. In May 1856, while Charles Sumner was delivering his "Crime Against Kansas" speech, proslavery men again marched on the city of Lawrence, this time burning business buildings and houses. Brown and his sons had been on their way to Lawrence when news of the invasion reached them. A short time later, they heard about the beating of Sumner in the Senate. Brown knew what he had to do. He took it upon himself to avenge the humiliation at Lawrence and the arrogance of the Sumner caning.

On Friday, May 23, the captain led four of his sons, his son-in-law, and two other volunteers on a secret mission to Potta-watomie Creek, not far from the Brown homestead. At midnight the next day, the band dragged five proslavery men from their homes in the region, brutally murdered them by slitting open their throats, and then mutilated their bodies. Later, Brown would say that the massacre had been "decreed by Almighty God, ordained from eternity."

Throughout Kansas, shock, horror, and some cheering greeted news of the bloody massacre. Proslavery people took the killings as an act of war, and proslavery newspapers printed detailed stories of the event along with cries for revenge. Many antislavery settlers condemned the atrocities but lay the blame at the feet of the proslavery forces who were trying to bully free staters out of Kansas. A massive hunt began for the "damn Browns" who had committed the murders, with wild bands of Missourians roaming the Pottawatomie region in search of the men. They would not be found. For now Brown entered a new phase of his antislavery career. He became an effective guerrilla commander known for his daring as well as his ruthlessness.

In one of his best-known exploits, Brown led a band of about thirty men against two hundred and fifty at a battle at Osawatomie. Mexican War veteran John W. Reid headed the proslavery forces. Although surrounded by Missourians, Brown and his men managed to escape and to kill a number of the enemy. They could not prevent the proslavery forces from burning Osawatomie, however. As Brown stood by, helplessly watching the town go up in flames, he turned to one of his sons with tears in his eyes. "I have only a short time to live — only one death to die," he said, "and I will die fighting for this cause."

It was after this battle that Brown began referring to himself as "John Brown of Osawatomie." He signed that name to a long, exaggerated account of the battle of Osawatomie that he wrote for Eastern newspapers, whose readers thrilled to the exploits of the fighting men in Kansas. Much of the legend of "Old Osawatomie Brown," as he became known, grew out of newspaper accounts both during his guerrilla days and later, when he stood trial for his life.

With the battle over, Brown began to look beyond Kansas to something bigger. New plans — God-given plans, he believed — were growing within him and he was ready for them now. The situation in Kansas was quieting down, too. A new governor, John W. Geary, managed to bring peace to the area and to control both proslavery and antislavery settlers. By 1858, Kansas would vote in a free election to adopt an antislavery constitution. Three years later, it would finally be admitted to the Union as a free state.

Between the time Brown left Kansas, at the end of 1856, to the time he launched his biggest campaign against slavery, a new event whipped Northerners and Southerners into a frenzy of excitement and distrust.

The event was the decision handed down by the United States Supreme Court in the case of *Dred Scott* v. *Sandford*. Scott had been the slave of one Dr. John Emerson of Missouri. Back in 1834, Emerson had taken Scott to the free state of Illinois and then to free territory in Wisconsin. Later Emerson took Scott back to the slave state of Missouri. In 1846, Scott sued for his freedom from a new master to whom he had been sold after Emerson's death on the grounds that having lived in free territory made him a free man. The case went from a circuit court to a state supreme court, and finally up to the United States Supreme Court, headed by Chief Justice Roger B. Taney.

The famous Dred Scott decision that the court gave in March 1857 convinced many Northerners that the Slave Power conspiracy that abolitionists had warned them about for years did, in fact, exist. The decision ruled that because Scott was a slave, he was not a citizen of the United States and therefore did not have the right to sue in federal court. Seven of the justices went even further. They recorded the opinion that the Missouri Compromise — repealed by the Kansas-Nebraska Act — had been unconstitutional, and that Congress could not exclude slavery from new territories.

Enraged by the proslavery decision, Republicans accused Taney of being in conspiracy with Stephen Douglas and President Buchanan, who had supported proslavery claims in Kansas. Northern newspapers warned that the next step the Slave Power would take would be to force slavery into all the states. Most outspoken and angry of the newspapers was the Republican *New York Tribune,* whose editor, Horace Greeley, had campaigned relentlessly against the spread of slavery into the territories. In many Northern states, abolitionists, Free Soilers, and citizens who belonged to no antislavery groups held Dred Scott Indignation meetings, and everywhere people talked about disunion. In this atmosphere of anger bordering on open violence, the schemes of John Brown would have looked attractive to thousands of Northerners who might otherwise have condemned him.

John Brown now set about getting the support of prominent citizens for a plan for widespread guerrilla warfare, a plan that was openly illegal and smacked of treason. After leaving Kansas, Brown headed for Boston, arriving there in January 1857. Quickly, he arranged to meet with the city's key abolitionists. Franklin B. Sanborn, a twenty-five-year-old schoolteacher, served as his contact. Young, impressionable, and romantic, Sanborn was secretary of the abolitionist Massachusetts Kansas

John Brown

Committee and was devoted to such antislavery men as Thomas
Higginson and Theodore Parker. Thrilled to meet Old Osawatomie Brown, who presented himself with letters of introduction, Sanborn immediately arranged for Brown to meet
Higginson, Parker, and other Boston abolitionists. Garrison
was among them. The two got along cordially, but could not
come to a meeting of the minds. Garrison had committed himself to the course of nonviolence. Brown was heading down
the trail of violence. They did not recognize the kinship between them.

Sanborn also introduced Brown to Dr. Samuel Gridley Howe and George Luther Stearns. A daring adventurer, Howe had fought in the Greek war for independence against Turkey and then come home to take up many reform causes. He had long been an active antislavery worker. His wife was Julia Ward Howe, one of the most respected women writers and social reformers of her day. Later, she would compose the words to "The Battle Hymn of the Republic." A tough Yankee businessman, Stearns prided himself on his antislavery activities and on his large contributions to Free Soil work in Kansas and to other abolitionist causes.

Out of Brown's meetings with the Boston men grew a special committee of six, dedicated to backing John Brown's plans for freedom: Stearns, Howe, Higginson, Parker, and Sanborn, along with Brown's old friend Gerrit Smith, the New York philanthropist. Later they would become known as the "Secret Six." For a long time, the committee did not know the details of Brown's plans. He spoke to them in vague terms of the continual need to guard against a new proslavery drive in Kansas. By the time he outlined his broader goals — the destruction of slavery through a massive slave uprising — the men had become too deeply involved with him, too hypnotized by his "flashing eyes," his courage, and his burning idealism, to turn back.

During the next two years, Brown worked out the plan for which he would always be remembered. After poring over maps of Southern territory, he decided to begin his full-scale war against slavery by attacking the federal arsenal at Harpers Ferry in western Virginia. Once he had captured that arsenal, he would have enough weapons to begin the most widespread slave revolt in history. Slaves from the area would flock to his side, he would arm them, and together they would take over the state. From there, they would spread the rebellion to the entire South, carrying on guerrilla warfare from the Allegheny Mountains, as he had once explained to Frederick Douglass.

Traveling about, trying to raise money and work out the details of his scheme, Brown began recruiting strong and angry young men to join him on the great day. He tried to get as many blacks as he could. He met with Frederick Douglass several times, once spending about two weeks in the Douglass home. Douglass felt great awe and sympathy for the white man. But as he learned more about Brown's plans, he knew that he wanted no part in them. At one point, not long before the attack, Brown met Douglass in a secret hiding place and pleaded with him, "Come with me, Douglass, I will defend you with my life. I want you for a special purpose . . ." But Douglass would not be moved.

Brown also tried to recruit Harriet Tubman. He met her in Chatham, Canada, where he held a convention of his followers in the spring of 1858. Deeply impressed with the determined, courageous woman, he wrote one of his sons that "*He Hariet* is the most of a *man* naturally; that I *ever* met with." She gave him information about Virginia, and promised to send him recruits, but she, too, refused to join his revolt.

At the Chatham convention, thirty-four blacks and twelve whites heard Brown read a "Provisional Constitution" that he had worked on for many months. It was a strange document, the blueprint for a government that Brown hoped to set up in territory he conquered. The constitution gave great power to its "Commander-in-Chief of the Army," who would run a kind of military dictatorship. In his mind, Brown saw himself as that military chief, running the country as he believed it ought to be run.

On the night of October 16, 1859, John Brown faced the band of faithfuls who were willing to fight and die for him. There were twenty-one in all, five of them blacks. Eighteen would go with him to his appointment with fate at Harpers Ferry. Three would remain behind at the farmhouse in Maryland that they had been using as their base of operations during the final stages of planning.

"Men, get on your arms; we will proceed to the Ferry," he told them solemnly. Like an Old Testament prophet, he was going out now to do the Lord's work.

Everything went smoothly at first. The men overcame the watchman at the armory easily. They made prisoners of whatever townspeople they saw in the street, and they rounded up some hostages from nearby areas. But even while Brown was congratulating himself on how well his plan was working, word of the invasion began to spread through the town. Church bells tolled and messengers rushed to send the alarm to neighboring villages. "Rebellion!" "Insurrection!" the messengers shouted as they ran. And the townspeople responded. Grabbing knives, axes, rifles, stones, or whatever they could lay hands on, they began to descend on the arsenal.

Brown should have gathered his men and retreated to the mountains, as his "general" John Kagi pleaded with him to do. But he refused to move. Was he waiting for slaves from the area to join him as he had always dreamed and planned they would? Was he holding out until he received a sign from God? Was he so dazed by the quick collapse of his rebellion that he could not move? No one would ever know. Brown and his men stayed put, moving only from the armory itself to the nearby fire-engine house. At one point, Brown sent his son Watson and another member of his band out to the growing hordes of townspeople with a white flag to negotiate a truce. The maddened mob gunned both of them down in cold blood. Watson managed to crawl back to the engine house, where he died at his father's feet.

By Tuesday morning, October 18, it was all over. A company of United States Marines sent out by President Buchanan and commanded by Colonel Robert E. Lee arrived in Harpers Ferry. The Marines broke through the thick oaken doors of the engine house, stormed the room, and captured Old Osawatomie and his men while the mobs that gathered outside shouted and cheered. By the time the raid on Harpers Ferry had ended, Brown had lost ten men, including two sons. Six men were taken captive with him, and five escaped. His band had killed a number of inhabitants of the town, among them the mayor.

At the Kennedy farm headquarters back in Maryland, militiamen found arms and pikes that the raiders had stored. They also found a carpetbag filled with letters and papers that had the names of Brown's secret conspirators and others whom he had tried to win to his cause.

Word of the would-be insurrection sent a feverish chill through the nation. For Southerners this was the end result they had always known would come from years of abolitionist agitation and Northern accusations. Gabriel, Denmark Vesey, Nat Turner — they had all been leading to this moment, the moment of open rebellion Southerners had dreaded all along.

With anger, hatred, near hysteria, Southerners screamed for blood and revenge, sure that John Brown was only part of a larger plot of insurrections that would now choke their land. At first Northerners viewed the Harpers Ferry event as the work of a madman. With a mixture of anger, amazement, and some awe, they feared that the "crazy fanatic" Brown had led them to the brink of war with the South. And many of them, too, wondered whether slave rebellions would now break out all over the South. Soon, horror and shock would give way to admiration and respect for Brown's bravery during his last days.

For the small group of prominent men who had aided him, John Brown's failure came as a blow that threatened to end their lives, too. The Secret Six who had backed Old Brown were stricken with panic. Why had he left that bag full of letters where he knew it could be captured? What other evidence had been left behind? The men scurried about, trying to cover their tracks and make their escapes. Gerrit Smith quickly burned all his own letters that had anything to do with Brown. Then he sent a member of his family to Boston and to Ohio, where John Brown, Jr., lived, to destroy as much evidence as he could find. Still, he trembled with terror, unable to eat or to sleep. Immediately after Brown was sentenced to death, Smith was confined to a state asylum for the insane. He was released shortly afterward, but continued to plead illness when called for questioning by a Senate investigating committee. Even years after the event, he refused to admit that he had had any knowledge of Brown's plans.

Howe confessed that he had helped Brown financially but explained that he had never expected anything so drastic to take place. Without waiting to be arrested, he and Stearns

escaped to Canada. Later, both returned to be questioned by
the Senate committee and managed to avoid giving direct answers to all questions relating to the raid. Sanborn, too, fled to
Canada immediately after the unsuccessful invasion. He returned within a few days, however. Then, when subpoenaed
like the others to appear before the Senate investigating committee, he fought off the marshal who delivered the subpoena.
After hearing that the Senate had voted to have him arrested,
he escaped to Canada again.

Parker had gone to Italy before the raid, and from there he
came out in support of Brown and slave rebellions. The bravest
of all, the fearless, dashing Higginson, refused to run or deny
his connection with Brown. "Is there no such thing as *honor*
among confederates?" he asked in disgust at the cowardice of
the others.

Although Frederick Douglass had not taken part in the conspiracy, his name was associated with Brown's. Friends warned
him that the New York governor might turn him over to the
Virginia authorities, who had trumped up charges against him.
So he, too, fled to Canada, and from there to England.

Brown's trial began in Virginia a little more than a week
after his capture. Newspapermen from all parts of the country
covered the proceedings, giving their readers detailed, often
sensational descriptions of Brown and all that he said. As the
days of the trial wore on, Northerners began to change their
minds about this man they had considered mad. He spoke with
calmness and courage. Sometimes his words sounded overdramatic, and sometimes they were too filled with his visions
of himself as the instrument of God. Always, however, they

John Brown arraigned before the court at Charlestown

rang with an unwavering conviction that slavery was evil and must be destroyed.

Northerners began to rally to Brown's defense, not so much to save his life as to glorify his goals. Many saw his death in the cause of slavery as having more meaning than his life ever could. Ralph Waldo Emerson hailed him as a saint whose death "will make the gallows glorious like the cross." Henry David Thoreau admitted, "I almost fear to hear of his deliverance, doubting if a prolonged life, if any life, can do as much as his death." Thoreau delivered a passionate "Plea for Captain John Brown" at Concord in which he said that it was Brown's "peculiar doctrine that a man has a perfect right to interfere by force with the slaveholder, in order to rescue the slave. I agree with him." Even William Lloyd Garrison finally broke with his lifelong principles of nonviolence. "I am prepared to say," he told a meeting in Brown's honor, after having agonized over the Harpers Ferry affair, " 'Success to every slave insurrection at the South, and in every slave country.' "

If Brown's admirers wished to make him a martyr, he was more than willing to help them. "I am worth inconceivably more to *hang* than for any other purpose," he told abolitionists who wanted to arrange an escape for him. He refused to have his lawyers enter a plea of insanity to save him from death. The lawyers went ahead anyway after the trial, collecting nineteen affidavits from relatives and friends saying that Brown had been insane at the time of the raid and that insanity ran in his family. Brown felt glad when the governor rejected the affidavits and refused to stop his execution.

The jury found Brown guilty as charged and he was sentenced to hang on the gallows a month later, on December 2. Shortly before being sentenced, he spoke words of eloquence that would be quoted for years to come. "I believe," he said, in speaking of God, "that to have interfered as I have done in behalf of His despised poor, is no wrong, but right. Now, if it is deemed necessary that I should forfeit my life for the furtherance of the ends of justice, and mingle my blood with the blood of millions in this country whose rights are disregarded by wicked, cruel, and unjust enactments, I say let it be done."

On the night of December 1, 1859, Mary Brown, John's wife of twenty-six years, came to say good-bye to her husband. The next morning, he left his jail cell under heavy guard. He was placed in a wagon and seated on top of the coffin in which he would be buried. Then he was taken to an open field where the gallows stood waiting for him. There, before a silent crowd, John Brown was hanged, while throughout the North church bells tolled and guns fired salutes to the martyred abolitionist.

As John Brown left his jail cell, he handed one of his attendants his last message to his country predicting that only with *"very much* bloodshed" would slavery be "purged away" from a *"guilty land."*

Years later, Frederick Douglass spoke about John Brown and the beginnings of the Civil War. "If we look over the dates, places and men," he said, ". . . we shall find that not Carolina, but Virginia, not Fort Sumter, but Harpers Ferry, and the United States Arsenal, not Major Anderson, but John Brown began the war that ended slavery and made this a free republic."

And as they marched into battle in that war, two years after his death, Northern troops sang: "John Brown's body lies a-mouldering in the grave . . . His soul goes marching on."

★ CHAPTER 15 ★

End of a Cause, Beginning of a Struggle

. . . I do order and declare that all persons held as slaves within said designated States and parts of States are, and henceforward shall be, free; and that the Executive Government of the United States, including the military and naval authorities thereof, shall recognize and maintain the freedom of said persons . . .

— Emancipation Proclamation,
signed by President ABRAHAM LINCOLN, January 1, 1863

★

For the most part, abolitionists welcomed the Civil War. After John Brown's martyrdom, they came to think, as he had, that only a final burst of violence would wrench the demon slavery from the soul of the nation.

Along with the rest of the country, the abolitionists had watched the national crisis reach the breaking point with the election of Abraham Lincoln on the Republican ticket in 1860. Even before Lincoln's election, a number of Southern states had announced that if he won, they would secede from the Union. By the time he took office, seven Southern states had left the Union and others were threatening to follow them. When Southerners fired on the federal Fort Sumter on April 12, 1861, the Civil War was on.

Abolitionists were divided in their feelings about Lincoln. Unlike the Radical Republicans (who had become their political allies in the antislavery cause) Lincoln was a moderate on the slavery issue. Although he personally hated slavery, he had never called for its outright abolition, and he had been willing to make concessions to the South to keep peace. During his famous debates with Stephen Douglas when the two were running for the U.S. Senate, Lincoln spoke against extending slavery to the territories, not for abolishing it. And in his inaugural address, he declared that he had no intention "directly or indirectly, to interfere with the institution of slavery where it exists." After the war broke out, he insisted again and again that he was leading the North in a life and death struggle to save the Union, not to end slavery. When Horace Greeley wrote an open letter to the President calling on him to emancipate the slaves, Lincoln replied: "If I could save the Union without freeing *any* slave I would do it, and if I could save it by freeing *all* the slaves I would do it; and if I could save it by freeing some and leaving others alone I would also do that."

Lincoln also believed, as Thomas Jefferson had before him, that the two races could not live in the same country. During the Civil War, he called a conference of leading blacks at which he spoke of a plan of gradual emancipation with compensation to slave owners and colonization of the freed blacks in Panama or Haiti. It was the old colonization idea that Garrison had fought thirty years earlier. The black leaders reacted now as they had then, by vehemently opposing the plan.

Unlike Lincoln, abolitionists viewed the war primarily as a struggle against slavery and were disturbed by Lincoln's attitudes and actions. Most outspoken in his opposition to Lincoln was Wendell Phillips, Garrison's closest friend for years. Phillips called Lincoln "The Slave Hound of Illinois" because of a proposal Lincoln had made in 1849. As part of a compromise with the South, the proposal called for the return to their masters of fugitives from the slave states caught in the District of Columbia. "I know Mr. Lincoln," Phillips once said. "He is a first rate, second rate man — that is all of him." Another time he complained that "Mr. Lincoln is not a leader . . . His theory of Democracy is that he is the servant of the people, not the leader." Garrison judged Lincoln less severely. He was deeply impressed with the President's strength and steadiness under pressure. Older and more mellow now, he was able to see another person's point of view and sympathize with his problems.

The President had many problems as the war progressed and pressures increased on him to free the slaves. Abolitionists and Radical Republicans did not let up for a moment in their campaign to obtain immediate freedom for all blacks. Douglass wrote, preached, and pleaded with the President for emancipation. Charles Sumner, now chairman of the Senate Committee on Foreign Relations, met with the Chief Executive often and used every opportunity he could to speak of the need for a statement of emancipation. Horace Greeley wrote powerful editorials in the *Tribune* in favor of emancipation, and Wendell Phillips traveled through the North rousing public opinion to the cause of freedom.

Lincoln remained cautious. He feared that freeing the slaves by Presidential proclamation would turn the border states against the North. Those states permitted slavery but were fighting on the Union side. He was not sure he had the legal

right under the Constitution to free the slaves. And he knew that he alone, and not a Douglass or a Phillips or a Greeley, had final responsibility for the war and the preservation of the Union.

The President moved slowly. After months of deliberation, on September 22, 1862, he issued a Preliminary Proclamation. It spoke of the possibility of compensated emancipation for slave owners in rebel states and of the President's support of colonization for those blacks who wanted to leave the country. Its main purpose, however, was to serve notice to the Confederate states that if they remained in rebellion after January 1, 1863, their slaves would be freed by proclamation.

Then, at last, came January and the final Emancipation Proclamation. Abolitionists had to admit among themselves that it was not all they would have wanted. The document freed the slaves only in those states that were in rebellion against the United States. Some 800,000 slaves in the border states were not freed. In addition, the President had made a point of declaring the Proclamation a "war measure," rather than a humanitarian decree. Its purpose was to help the North defeat the Southern armies by winning slaves to its side. Still, the Emancipation Proclamation became one of the landmarks in the history of America. For all its shortcomings, it gave joy and hope to millions of black men, women, and children, whom it declared were free. And it served as a symbol to people all over the world that the United States stood by the principles of its Declaration of Independence.

In spite of their reservations, abolitionists hailed the document, which they saw as official recognition of their labors and sacrifices. Some of those who had fought the antislavery battle for years, such as James G. Birney and Theodore Parker, had not lived to enjoy this moment. Others, such as Theodore Weld and the Grimké sisters, had long since retired into private life. But the many who had devoted themselves to the end, could glory now in their time of victory.

In the Boston Music Hall hundreds of the city's notables gathered on January 1, 1863, to await the signing of the document. When word came that the President had issued his Proclamation, the crowd went wild.

"Three cheers for Garrison!" someone called out.

In the balcony, William Lloyd Garrison stood up and faced the audience. He could see John Greenleaf Whittier, Ralph Waldo Emerson, Henry Wadsworth Longfellow, and many other elite of New England. He stood quietly while people all around applauded him. It was the proudest moment of his life.

In another part of Boston, in Tremont Temple, nearly three thousand men and women, many of them black, came together for the announcement of the Proclamation. With the news of its release, people laughed and cried and danced for joy. Then Frederick Douglass rose, and in a deep baritone voice began to sing the hymn "Blow Ye the Trumpet, Blow." Thousands of voices joined him. It was the hymn John Brown loved and sang often while he held his children on his knee. And it was the hymn his neighbors had sung as his coffin was lowered into its grave.

The scenes in Boston were repeated in towns and cities all over the North. Songs and cheers of happiness hailed the signing of the Emancipation Proclamation, making the bloody battlefields of the war seem like an unreal nightmare.

But the fighting was real, and for a long time the Union Army suffered defeats and poor commands. At first the President hesitated to accept blacks in the army. By 1862, however, black men were beginning to serve in fighting units of their own, and to be armed like their white comrades. After the Proclamation, recruiters went through the North and those parts of the South that had been taken by the Union armies, inviting blacks to enlist. Frederick Douglass, an enthusiastic recruiter, ran ads in his newspaper calling his people to war: "Men of Color, to Arms!" the ads cried. His first recruits were his sons Charles and Lewis. Douglass also used his influence to get better treatment for black enlistees than they had received at the beginning, working especially to give them equal pay with whites.

Thomas Wentworth Higginson went further than most abolitionists in helping the war cause and black recruits. He gave up his parish, enlisted in the service, and took command of an all-black regiment, which was the first Union regiment made up of former slaves.

Other abolitionists contributed to the war effort in their own ways. Most of them were too old to fight themselves, but they had sons and relatives who fought and died in the war they had helped bring on.

By the time the war ended in 1865, the abolitionists — once the most despised members of their society — had become heroes to their countrymen. People who had ignored the abolitionists or ranted against them in the prewar years now suddenly were happy to recall their own contributions and heroic deeds in the antislavery struggle. "New anti-slavery friends are becoming as plenty as roses in June," wrote Lydia

Maria Child to Garrison. "Sometimes, when they tell me they have always been anti-slavery, I smile inwardly, but I do not contradict the assertion; I merely marvel at their power of keeping a secret so long!"

For Garrison, the end of the war meant the end of a cause. The Thirteenth Amendment, abolishing slavery throughout the United States, was close to ratification when he told members of the American Anti-Slavery Society: "We organized expressly for the abolition of slavery; we called our Society an *Anti-Slavery* Society." Now, he went on, the society's work had ended, "swallowed up in the great ocean of popular feeling against slavery." The time had come to disband.

The proposal brought a break between Garrison and his life-long friend Phillips. The break had been coming during the war years, as Garrison became a more enthusiastic supporter of Lincoln and Phillips continued to attack the President. The

Thomas W.
Higginson

division deepened as the war drew to a close. Phillips and a number of old Garrisonians spoke of using the antislavery society as a base for achieving other rights for blacks, especially the right to vote. Garrison had doubts about giving the freed slaves the vote without a period of rehabilitation and education. That had never been a goal of their crusade, he argued. For him, political aims had always been less important than moral ones.

The dispute between the two men grew bitter and heated. Finally, Garrison resigned from the antislavery society and Phillips was elected president in his place. It was a sad moment, even for those who opposed him, when Garrison stood before members of the American Anti-Slavery Society, thanked them for the honor of having been president for many years, and told them: "I never should have accepted the post if it had been a popular one. I took it because it was unpopular; because we, as a body, were everywhere denounced . . . To-day, it is popular to be President of the American Anti-Slavery Society. Hence my connection with it terminates here and now . . . I bid you an affectionate adieu." Shortly afterward, in December 1865, Garrison published his last issue of the *Liberator*. As a fitting end, it carried the news that the Thirteenth Amendment had been ratified.

Although Garrison broke with Phillips, he joined Phillips, Douglass, Lydia Maria Child, and other former abolitionists in supporting their old friends the Radical Republicans in their fight with the administration of President Andrew Johnson after the assassination of Lincoln. The Radicals opposed the lenient reconstruction terms Johnson, like Lincoln, proposed for the defeated Southern states. For a variety of reasons —

idealism mixed with politics — the Radicals wanted to limit the rights of Southern whites and to extend broad rights to the newly freed blacks.

The old abolitionists had little respect for Andrew Johnson. They had expected him to take a firm stand against the South and were amazed and disappointed when he chose to follow a soft line. "My spirit is greatly tried by Andy Johnson," said Lydia Maria Child, expressing the feelings of many former abolitionists. When the Radicals prepared to impeach Johnson, the antislavery people fully supported them. Few had any real understanding of politics or of the far-reaching power struggle between Congress and the Presidency that the attempted impeachment represented. The abolitionists did not see, and, if they did, they did not care, that many of the Radicals wanted to give freed slaves the vote and take voting rights away from Southern whites less out of concern for black people than as a way of maintaining their own political power. For Phillips, Douglass, and the others, the issue of black suffrage was becoming more important than anything.

Before that goal was accomplished, the abolitionist band had one more deep split among themselves. Once again, the problem centered on women. Elizabeth Cady Stanton, Susan B. Anthony, and other women's rightists had worked hard for the antislavery cause. During the abolition struggle, they had made their own cause secondary to the cause of the black man. Now they wanted to pick up where they had left off, and they demanded of their male coworkers that women's suffrage be put ahead of black suffrage in the list of causes still to be won. Frederick Douglass and other black and white antislavery leaders put the women down, insisting that while the vote was desirable for them, it was crucial for the survival of the blacks in white America. Defeated, the women formed their own women's suffrage organizations. Another fifty years would pass before the Nineteenth Amendment to the Constitution would give women the vote.

The Fifteenth Amendment, guaranteeing the vote to citizens of the United States regardless of race or color, was ratified on March 30, 1870, during the administration of Ulysses S. Grant. Ten days later, the American Anti-Slavery Society held its final meeting. Phillips presided over a skeleton of the former organization that included Lucretia Mott, Stephen Foster, Frederick Douglass, and other old-time abolitionists. Everybody missed Garrison, who had broken all contact with the society. With emotion and amidst applause, Phillips announced that the American Anti-Slavery Society was disbanded, and "our long work is sealed."

The work had been long and hard. The battle was ended. But years after the abolitionists disappeared from public life, questions about them remained. What had they really accomplished? Had they helped rid the country of slavery or had they actually hindered the antislavery cause? Should they be blamed for causing the Civil War, or should they be praised for freeing the blacks?

In the years immediately after the Civil War, the reputation of the abolitionists was at an all-time high. Northerners looked upon them as elder statesmen who had warned against the evils of slavery and foreseen the national catastrophe that would result from it. Once despised, they were treated with great respect and numerous books and articles were published in praise of them.

Then, with the end of Reconstruction, they fell into disfavor, as they had been during all the years of their struggle. A busy, growing nation had lost interest in the "Negro problem" and those who had tried to solve it. By the early 1900s, historians were speaking of the Civil War as a bloodbath that could have been avoided had national emotions not burst out of bounds. They accused the abolitionists of stirring violence with their harsh language and their wholesale attacks on slaveholders. By angering and frightening the South, critics said, abolitionists had forced Southerners into a more extreme proslavery position than they might otherwise have taken, and in that way they had hurt their own cause. "Irresponsible," "emotionally sick," "the lunatic fringe" were some of the labels slapped on the abolitionists.

Today, more than a century after the Civil War, when problems of civil rights and race relations stand out among the most pressing problems of our society, the work and aims of the abolitionists have taken on a new light. Behind their extremist language and their shrill emotionalism lay ideals of freedom and equality that have as much meaning now as they did more than a hundred years ago. And for all their shortcomings, the abolitionists did succeed in changing history. They left behind them a heritage of achievements — and problems — that still influence our lives.

The abolitionists raised their voices against slavery at a time when a conspiracy of silence hung over the country. Slavery was a way of life, deeply entrenched and even safeguarded by the Constitution. Few people thought about it, and fewer still talked about it. Those who did object to the institution spoke in hushed tones so as not to offend slaveholders or interfere with the property rights of others. The abolitionists crashed through that wall of silence with words and slogans designed to shatter old ideas and prejudices.

The emotional language of the abolitionists was not simply the expression of excited personalities. Like militants of other times, they presented their goals in extremist terms meant to shock their countrymen and shake them out of their indifference. "Urge immediate abolition as earnestly as we may," wrote William Lloyd Garrison, "it will be gradual abolition in the end." Only by demanding everything, the abolitionists believed, would they gain anything at all.

The violent language used by the abolitionists in their attacks on slavery aroused violent reactions. They were mobbed and beaten, tarred and feathered, and, in the case of Elijah Lovejoy, murdered. Yet, instead of stopping the abolitionists, the attacks spurred them on and strengthened their cause. Men and women with no commitment against slavery felt sympathy for the abolitionist martyrs and feared for the civil liberties of all Americans. By coupling the struggle against slavery with the constitutional right of freedom of speech, the abolitionists made their first inroads to the public's consciousness and conscience.

The men and women who made up the abolitionist ranks were products of their own times and backgrounds. Like the early Puritans from whom many were descended, they were stern people for the most part. Moral lessons filled their writings and speeches, with seldom a touch of humor. For relaxation, they sang hymns and read the Bible. Many opposed smoking, drinking, and even the theater. A good proportion came from substantial, proper families and had extensive education. Few among the white abolitionists had experienced personal contact with slavery or firsthand knowledge of how the slave system worked. It was the institution of slavery as a whole that they fought rather than the misery of individual slaves. They opposed slavery on principle because it took away the humanity of both slave and master — degrading the slave and brutalizing his owner. It was as important for slaveholders to free their slaves, they said, as it was for the slaves to become free.

Behind the abolitionists' war on slavery lay deep religious convictions. They lived in an age when religion dominated men's thoughts and actions. Religious revivalists toured the country converting people to a life of good works and Christian piety. Like the evangelical preachers, the abolitionists manned their crusade to convert their countrymen to an acceptance of freedom for everyone, black as well as white. Again and again they emphasized the sinfulness of slavery and called on both Northerners and Southerners to repent. Even in later years, when many abolitionists turned to political action, the view of slavery as a moral and religious problem remained an essential part of the antislavery movement.

In the end, their moral warfare was successful. Gradually, they saw their ideas seep through, layer by layer, into the mainstream of American thought. In 1830, when they began their struggle, each abolitionist plea was like a voice crying in the wilderness. By 1860, the antislavery voices had swelled into a chorus of protest that echoed through the free states. Many political and economic events, apart from the abolitionists' own work, helped spread antislavery sentiments. But it was the abolitionists who first aroused the nation to the cause of the slave and made it the most crucial issue of their time. Had they not done so, slavery might have continued much longer than it did. With the Civil War and the end of slavery, the abolitionists could claim victory in their difficult crusade.

But the story of the abolitionists is not a simple success story. It involved heartbreak and compromise and failure along with success. The abolitionists began their crusade with a firm commitment to nonviolence. As time went on and slavery continued, they moved further and further away from that commitment, doubting whether they would ever accomplish anything without force. Eventually, they made a saint of the most violent man among them, John Brown. And their final victory came in a burst of violence that was the Civil War.

Over the years, as they grew more desperate in their cause, the abolitionists also went from criticizing slave laws to openly disobeying the laws of the land, and then to attacking the United States Constitution. They made civil disobedience a philosophy of life and based their actions on the higher law that dwelled within themselves.

The danger of the higher-law doctrine for the abolitionists and for those who later followed them lies in the many interpretations to which it lends itself. For William Lloyd Garrison, the higher law, with its emphasis on the individual and his own conscience, meant a denial of all government and all institutions, a kind of anarchy in which no nation can exist. For John Brown, the higher law meant freedom to stir up a slave insurrection, even if its consequences might destroy the nation. Since the days of the abolitionists, many groups, of both the right and the left, have used the higher-law argument as justification for their own beliefs and opinions, leading to actions that sometimes have helped and sometimes have hurt society and the people in it.

With their civil disobedience, their higher law, and their continuous agitation against slavery, the abolitionists contributed to the national crisis that led to the Civil War. They did not cause the war, as some critics have accused them of doing. A variety of social, economic, and political differences that had long divided the country worked together to bring on that final explosion. The words and deeds of the abolitionists, however, added to the ferment of the times in which it became inevitable for one part of the nation to take up arms against the other.

For all the militancy of their struggle against slavery, the abolitionists were not prepared for the Civil War or its results. Their goal all along had been to make Americans sit up and listen and then change their ways, rather than to plan the details of emancipation. They had cried out for freedom for the slave, but they had not thought out solutions to the problems that freedom would bring to the former slaves and former masters. They had preached equality for blacks, but they had not worked out ways to guarantee them an equal place in American society. When freedom came they retired from the scene, satisfied that they had seen their crusade to a successful finish. Their lack of foresight had consequences whose effects can still be felt.

At the end of the chaotic period of Reconstruction, blacks began to sink once again under restrictions and oppressions not far removed from their slave days. In the South, Black Laws kept them tightly "in their place." Grandfather clauses, literacy tests, and poll taxes prevented them from entering voting booths. Organizations such as the Ku Klux Klan terrorized them into submission and quiet desperation. In the North, whites ignored the increasing poverty and poor living conditions of blacks. Few jobs were made available, except the lowest paying and most menial. Black children attended segregated, usually inferior, schools. Few blacks could go on to college or enter professions.

The abolitionists had succeeded in their goal of abolishing slavery. But they had failed to realize that achieving real freedom for black people would require much more than merely ending slavery.

Books to Read

Douglass, Frederick. *Life and Times of Frederick Douglass.* New York, 1892.

Franklin, John Hope. *From Slavery to Freedom.* New York, 1967.

Nelson, Truman (editor). *Documents of Upheaval: Selections from William Lloyd Garrison's "The Liberator."* New York, 1966.

Oates, Stephen B. *To Purge This Land with Blood: A Biography of John Brown.* New York, 1970.

Petry, Ann. *Harriet Tubman: Conductor on the Underground Railroad.* New York, 1955.

Quarles, Benjamin. *Black Abolitionists.* New York, 1969.

Still, William. *The Underground Railroad.* Philadelphia, 1872.

Stowe, Harriet Beecher. *Uncle Tom's Cabin.* New York, 1938.

Thomas, John L. *The Liberator: William Lloyd Garrison.* Boston, 1963.

Truth, Sojourner. *Narrative of Sojourner Truth.* Chicago, 1970 (reprint of 1875 edition).

We are grateful to The Bettmann Archive, Inc.,
for permission to include the photographs found on
pages 14, 33, 35, 52, 83, 95, 100, 121, 122, 128,
142, 148, 166, 169, 176, and 183; and to Culver
Pictures, Inc., for the photographs on pages 27, 46, 57,
60, 64, 72, 87, 132, 144, 152, 157, 189, and 193.

INDEX